Lady
and the Tribe

How to Create Empowering
Friendship Circles

Brenda Billings Ridgley

**Lady and The Tribe: How to Create Empowering
Friendship Circles**
Published by Whole You Media
Denver, CO

ISBN 978-1737289708
Personal Growth / Happiness

Cover and interior design by Victoria Wolf,
wolfdesignandmarketing.com. Copyright owned by
Brenda Ridgley.

Whole You Media

Parker, I am not sure if you know this, but I think that you are the kindest man I have ever met. It's no surprise why every person who has ever met you instantly likes you given your undeniable charm. You are an amazing father and the "cool" uncle that all our nieces and nephews adore. We all really do love you jokes, especially the "Handsomest Dad Award" that the kids have won at every event … for decades. You and I have been through some hard times but came through them stronger. I feel loved, understood and confident in our "us" and that is because of you. Ultimately, as long as we are side by side, I know everything will be alright. I'm blessed to call you, my husband. *I love you.*

CONTENTS

FOREWORD

*"Many tribes of a modern kind doing brand new work…
same spirit by side, Joining hearts and hands in ancestral
twine…" Spirit Bird, She flies.*

Spirit Bird, Xavier Rudd

WHEN BRENDA CALLED to ask me what I thought of her inspiration for the title of her first book, *Lady and The Tribe,* I had no idea (and probably neither did she) that she would immediately be inviting me to offer the Forward. Really it was that Brenda's intuition and wisdom tickled her sensitivity to how her Native American "sister" might view and react to the now culturally popular use of the word "Tribe."

Having grown up in rural North Texas in the eighties, where the town was effectively still segregated, I was constantly asked, "What ARE you? Are you Mexican? Are you Indian? I suppose I knew that I was "something" because I was definitely NOT like the other pre-teens in my middle school. They were White. Or Black.

I was poor and lived on the wrong side of the railroad tracks dividing the town. My mother was not married. Not Catholic. So, not White.

I was a diligent student. Perfect grammar. No good at any sport. Smooth wavy brown hair and slight build. Not Baptist. Definitely not Black.

Truth was, I wondered more than them, what I was.

What I did know was that I didn't know. I had this longing in my soul to belong though. To know… and be known… for WHO, not WHAT, I was… to be a part of the group, a piece of the puzzle and inside the circle of trust. And every step, twist, and turn of my wandering life was unknowingly weaving the connection of my "WHO am I" question to finding my Tribe. Literally.

There are some soul level things about us all that just honestly ARE embedded in our DNA. Discovering my Lakhota heritage has been a wild ride and still is. Honoring our ancestral programming is more of a spiritual journey than any religious training program might lead us to believe. There are mysteries of how our Creator works that we and our science are just not qualified to explain. Matching up our invisible, unexplainable traits to our cultural-environmental training is the stuff that decades of life, and therapy, are made of. We find answers to our own questions of the soul when we hold them up to the mirrors of our circles. Essentially, aren't we all just searching for who we are by finding our Tribe?

In many Native traditions, the Spirit Bird represents the submission of The Will to The Wind.

Tribes of all indigenous nations look up to the sky to locate their Spirit Bird for direction from The Divine Creator. And sometimes, The Creator sends Spirit Bird to us when we are not looking up.

What is the wind and weather today? Which direction is safe to travel? What is the sun and light path to follow? Will you intercede for me in the highest places? Carry my prayers on your wings across the mountains. Join me and honor my ceremonies. Give me wisdom to lead my Tribe.

Brenda is both. The Lady ... and the Tribe. You will see that as her story is unpacked. The gift of connecting many Tribes from the Divine perspective is embodied in the chapters to follow. Whatever your life season: planting or harvest, seeking or finding, question or answer ... you will discover the themes of the modern Tribe and its calling to you to remember who and what you are ... or to find out, if you've always wanted to know.

Brenda shows us the answer is found in joining our hearts and hands in ancestral twine and stokes the ceremonial fires within us to want to do that—for ourselves, for each other, and for the greater good of the Tribe.

For those reasons, I am honored to offer a Lakhota blessing over the title she's chosen. And bless the honor of knowing what I am and my part in the Tribe.

Wopila, Wakan Takan kici un
Thanks given for all of existence and the blessing inherent in each moment of it.
May the Great Spirit and Creator God bless you.

~Michelle Eileen

CHAPTER 1:

Awakening

YOU ARE ABOUT to embark on a journey that can fill the space inside your soul that is longing for more. You may have no idea why you feel empty, but you know something is missing. What is it that is preventing you from becoming the best "whole" version of yourself?

Believe it or not, the missing link involves our lack of meaningful connection to other human beings. You may be thinking, "Oh no . . . that's not me! I have lots of friends! I have so many friends, I can't even manage to interact with them as often as I'd like!" That very well may be true. However, it is not the quantity but rather the quality of these friendships that matters. In the chapters ahead, we will discuss what it means to find, deepen, build, preserve, and broaden friendships so that they become like family—your soul sisters. When three or more of you gather together, you are a Tribe.

Today, a dichotomy exists between our concurrent hyper connectedness—the immediate and ongoing ability to check up on faraway friends via social media—and our elevated sense of emotional alienation. Add to that, we as a culture are so focused on career success, financial accomplishments, and family milestones that we often lack the time and energy to connect with others beyond those arenas. Despite being surrounded by people, places and things, somehow we are left feeling alone. We are not alone because we lack relationships. We are alone because these relationships lack depth, knowledge, and certainty. In his column, "Loneliness is Killing Us," George Monbiot suggests that, much as we labeled the Stone Age, Iron Age, Space Age, and Information Age, this era will be called "The Age of Loneliness."[1]

Almost without noticing, we have distanced ourselves from the people who *choose* to love us without obligation. These closest personal friendships are ever present—yet do not demand our time. They are an advocate in our corner, mirroring back to us who we really are. This neglect is not without a price. We must actively seek, grow, and maintain these relationships. If we fail, we won't just lose a friend—we'll lose a piece of ourselves.

The wonderful thing is that no matter where you are right now with your relationships, you can exponentially improve your connections by deciding to give them a little more attention and intention.

Loneliness Can Be Lethal

Since we live in this global, socially connected world, how is it possible for anyone to be lonely? Psychologically speaking, loneliness does not necessitate social isolation. Being lonely means feeling detached from others yet having the desire for a connection or a relationship.

Medically speaking, the feeling of isolation raises levels of stress hormones in the bloodstream and may play a role in firing up chronic inflammation, a risk factor in heart disease, diabetes, and even some forms of cancer. Dr. Douglas Nemeck, chief medical officer for behavioral health at Cigna, states that loneliness has the same impact on mortality as smoking 15 cigarettes a day, making it even more dangerous than obesity. The problem has reached *epidemic* proportions, rivaling the risks posed by tobacco and the nation's ever-expanding waistline.[2] Relationships can affect your health both for the good and bad. However, solitude can make you sick![3]

- Do you feel exhausted, no matter how much sleep you get? You just never feel caught up?
- Are you eating like a bird but still gaining weight?
- Do you have trouble concentrating?
- Are you a bit depressed and/or experiencing anxiety?
- Do you often feel stressed out?
- Are you plagued with insomnia?

These symptoms, as well as disease and premature death, can be the result of too few friendships. For the most part, we are not lonely because we don't know people. We are lonely because the majority of our relationships lack the depth, ease, and intimacy we crave.

The millennial generation has been called the loneliest generation because their tech-savvy communication habits result in a lack of physical connection. A 2018 nationwide survey by Texas A&M Health found that nearly half of Americans report feeling alone or left out, and one in four Americans rarely feel as though there are people who really understand them.[4] Individually, we are more isolated as a nation than ever before.

Now consider what those loneliness numbers would look like today. During the pandemic, we were directed to quarantine from anyone outside of our household for weeks or months at a time. We were encouraged to 'socially distance' and keep six feet away from others. Many of us were furloughed from work, losing our routine of water cooler chitchat and after-work happy hours. Others were sent home to work remotely for the first time. We were required to wear masks that made communicating difficult.

The masks, in my observation, also created a disconnection from who we really are. We could go about our day in *stealth mode*. What is stealth mode? Well, on occasion when I go into a grocery store without my hair and makeup done—let's call it the *natural* look—I pretend no one can see me, and I dart in and out without engaging with anyone. During the pandemic, we basically lived our lives in stealth mode, limiting social interactions, and with that, often our good manners. In my opinion, many people behave differently when they wear a mask.

Although you cannot see a covered smile, you can still recognize a warm greeting in someone's eyes. You can still share a hello and nod of acknowledgement when socially distancing and/or wearing a mask. However, stealth mode disconnected us from our normal societal etiquette and upbringing. I hope that you reserve your stealth mode for occasional use only! I also hope that you are faring better than the 50% or more of people in the United States who are lonely.[5]

Meredith Williamson, PhD, clinical assistant professor at the Texas A&M College of Medicine explains that loneliness has been linked to many different health issues like depression and risk of high blood pressure. Additionally, obesity and alcohol and drug abuse are common.[6]

There are three different types of relationships that someone experiencing loneliness could be lacking: intimate, relational and collective.[7]

1. Intimate relationships are usually in reference to a spouse or significant other.
2. Relational relationships refer to ones' network of close friends and relatives.
3. Collective relationships are those that involve a group that one is affiliated with and one's general connection to society.

Here are some facts on the health risks of loneliness as reported by the Campaign to End Loneliness Organization.[8]

Loneliness:
- Is likely to increase your risk of death by 26% (Holt-Lunstad, 2015)
- Is a risk factor for depression later in life
- Can be associated with early mortality (when linked to severe depression)
- Puts individuals at greater risk of cognitive decline and dementia (when coupled with social isolation)

Loneliness can also become a chronic condition as reported in an article "Signs and Symptoms of Chronic Loneliness" released by Cigna in March of 2019.[9] This occurs when feelings of loneliness and uncomfortable social isolation go on for a long period of time. It is characterized by a constant and unrelenting feeling of being alone, separated or divided from others, and an inability to connect on a deeper level. It can also be accompanied by deeply rooted feelings of inadequacy, poor self-esteem, and self-loathing.

Why is loneliness so lethal? As human beings, one of our greatest needs is to be seen, acknowledged, and cared for. We want to belong and be a part of something larger than ourselves. More so than men, women need to maintain close connections. Relationships increase serotonin and oxytocin, the bonding hormone. In times of stress, women don't just experience the drive toward fight or flight—they also release oxytocin. This hormone surge can compel women to "tend and befriend."[10] Research is clear. Close friendships are necessary for optimal health and well-being. A longitudinal study of aging found that strong social networks lengthen survival among older people. Dr. Amir Leving suggests that social connections are the most powerful way for us to regulate our emotional distress and that proximity to someone you are securely attached to is the most effective way to calm yourself.[11]

An article in the New York Times reported that close relationships create positive mental and physical reactions in our body, mind, and heart.[12] We are less likely to experience high levels of loneliness when we feel supported by intimate and close relationships. Strong relationships with close friends or family benefit us greatly and fulfil our social needs.

Great Expectations

Regardless of the condition of your current relationships, your friendships are an area of your life that could probably benefit from a little more attention. There has got to be at least one person in every Tribe who takes the lead to make things happen and stay connected. However, for a Tribe to be effective, the efforts must be reciprocal, and each individual must add value to the group. In the chapters ahead, we are going to take a deep dive into all things Tribe—the family you choose. This will include:

1. The depth that many women are missing in their relationships
2. How superficial friendships may be hurting us
3. How building trust and intimacy with a few girlfriends may improve your health, well-being, and longevity
4. How to be a good friend.
5. How to create depth in friendships.
6. How to be the leader of your Tribe
7. And much more.

Thank you for taking the first step in this journey by picking up this book. My goal is to uplift all women with the power of connection. With your participation in this movement, you can make a difference not only in your own life, but in the lives of those around you. Wherever you are right now, you can find a more rewarding and joyful life with your own Tribe. Let's get started.

CHAPTER 2:

The Lady

FIRST AND FOREMOST, the priority of this work is *the woman*. The Lady and her journey to wholeness. We will use the tree of life as an analogy of our own individual being. The goal of this work is to guide the Lady to discover her own joy and happiness through friendship and connection.

The Roots that Nourish and Anchor

Our parents provided the seed and soil for our trees of life. Our internal environment—genetics, traits, and characteristics—all stem from the seed. The soil is our external environment. It includes the lessons we were taught, the role models we observed, and the experiences that created our values, ethics, and morals. It also includes where we lived and the individuals and activities to whom we were introduced. Everything about us literally stems from nature and nurture.

Each of us has our own story. Our foundations, soils, and terroirs host our anchoring roots and set the stage for our beings, our individual trees of life. Throughout *Lady and the Tribe*, I will be sharing my own story, as well as the stories of other women, to illustrate journeys of personal growth and friendship.

Brenda

I was the firstborn of three in a traditional midwestern family. My loving parents were success-driven and wanted to create a new life for themselves. My mother was raised in a farming family, and my father's father made his living as a head chef in a veteran's hospital. My parents were success-driven, and although they never spoke of it, I believe they wanted to create their own legacy. Both of my parents were first generation college graduates, and both earned their master's degrees after I was born. Mom and Dad had big dreams, and they began their journey by moving from Iowa and Kansas—where they were raised—to the exciting and new Colorful Colorado.

My parents advanced regularly in their careers, beginning as teachers and growing into corporate America and the world of finance. Their success was impressive, and I remember my grandparents beaming with pride as they paraded their son and daughter at church when we visited. Theirs was the generation that broke the mold of the typical American family where the husband was the breadwinner and the wife stayed home to manage the household and raise the family. Whether it was born of ambition, necessity, or more likely both, their rapid career advancement did not come without a price.

I know my mother was not alone in her new paradigm shifting, backbreaking role as *Superwoman*. This generation of moms had insurmountable and unrealistic responsibilities. They were the first to work full time while still being expected to cook and take care of the kids, household, and husband. I remember my mom rushing around the house, serving the family dinner, then cleaning up and moving on to other chores like laundry and housekeeping. For a time, I remember my father going to the living room after dinner to watch TV while my mother continued to work.

I realize this is making my father out to be the bad guy, but I really don't blame him. In their new reality, I believe women found themselves propelled to be everything to everyone. Since they were fighting for equal rights in all things, they had to show strength and prove that they needed no help to *do the job* well. The men weren't really seeking this change in roles. They only wanted the same benefits of marriage that they had witnessed from their parents growing up. They watched their fathers go to work each day and come home in time for a home-cooked meal created by the homemaker, his loving wife. He would then relax a bit in the study reading or watching television before bed.

It is not surprising that men in this new reality, where both husband and wife worked full time, continued to behave as they had seen their fathers do growing up. Especially when his wife had *Superwoman* expectations of herself. She also was likely feeling guilty about missing time with her kids and always feeling behind on the household chores. These expectations, of themselves and others, were a recipe for disaster and not sustainable. It is no wonder that divorce, once almost unheard of, spiked in the 1970s. This was the defining decade for divorce as America reached 1,193,062 divorces in 1979.[13]

As the oldest, I remember personally watching my parents struggle. This included more than a few arguments. I watched them work through this pretty sizable distinction in point of view. In various levels of intensity, they expressed their needs and frustrations, listened, negotiated, and came out united, stronger than before. This book is not about marriage, however, my parents are great role models who showed me what it takes to find, maintain, and enhance our closest and most important connections. They showed me that you must put in the work. Relationships are not easy but are *oh-so* rewarding. This, in part, is why I eagerly seek to build strong friendships in my own life.

My parents' dream to succeed became a reality. They earned more money and a lifestyle beyond what they had experienced growing up. Dad had all the latest and greatest toys, including a new sports car every year or so and a country club membership. He even had his own airplane that he learned to fly. He encouraged my mother to also become a pilot, so they could fly across the country together with me and my siblings in-tow.

As my parents created their lifestyle, they would go hunting for a new home every few years. Each time they would "upgrade" to a bigger home in a nicer neighborhood. I can remember living in five different homes before I was 18. Each time we moved, this meant a new school, new friends, and a new start, socially speaking. In seventh grade, we moved in the middle of first semester. At the time I didn't think too much of it because I had done it before. Looking back, however, I remember suddenly having a strong desire to fit in and be included. I sought to belong to a group of friends who had spent years developing relationships through play dates, school, activities, and church.

I believe that my socially formative years shaped me to become sensitive to exclusion, strongly desiring inclusivity in all things, and to place a high value on belonging. That is why I am passionate about seeking, developing, and nurturing meaningful relationships today.

The Branches that Lift and Support

Our closest friendships become the branches of our tree of life. These relationships strongly resemble tree branches because they grow stronger with time and attention. They hold you up in high regard and stay strong with the winds of change. As the seasons of your life pass through, the branches of your relationships remain growing, supportive, and ready to lift you higher the next season.

I have been able to build some pretty deep and amazing relationships in my lifetime, one dating back to junior high school and newer members within the last decade. I am honored to introduce you to my loving Tribe:

1. Sis: My beautiful and clever little sister who is spontaneous, always up for an adventure, and I know I can count on her. Sis, without exception, has my back and is an encourager.
2. Homegirl: BFFs since Jr. High (she feels like home to me).
3. Bestie: My comrade, champion, and guardian. She is always on board with my shenanigans, and she *just gets me.*
4. Soul Seraph: Wise and centered cherub who brings peace, love, and serenity wherever she goes.
5. Ms. Magnanimous: Loveable and loyal friend from high school; "like family"—a friend for life.

You will be introduced to each of them, and a few other remarkable women, in the friendship stories within these chapters.

My Tribe today, including me, rounds to an even six. There is no right, wrong, or even best number of members in a Tribe. My Tribe truly lifts me up with encouragement, affirmation, and love. They give me strength when I am weak, push me when I want to give up, and cheer me on when I am succeeding. They are loyal and true to me. I completely trust their intentions and know that they have my best interest at heart. They have been with me through failure and triumph, as I have been for them. I am a better wife, mother, and contributor to my community because of these rewarding relationships.

Bobbi

I cannot wrap up a chapter about "The Lady" and my upbringing without sharing more about my sister. As you would imagine, Bobbi is a huge part of my own story. We have witnessed life together and taught each other lessons of sisterly love. We have grown side by side like vines on a wall, weaving together and apart as we reach for our best lives.

My little sister, Bobbi, used to charmingly run up to me and give me big squeezes when we were kids. I have never been a big fan of PDA (public displays of affection). I would often peel her off of me as if I were just covered in slime, with an air of repugnance. My mother would scold me, telling me how lucky I was to have such an adoring little sister. Mom was right.

Growing up, I would say we were companions more than friends, and that was my fault. As we moved around every few years through grade school, my priority was to try to fit in and make new friends. Having an annoying little sister following me around all the time was not cool. I would ditch her and exclude her from activities with my new friends. Having had my share of feeling "left out" as the new kid, maybe I was overcompensating and creating my own exclusive clique.

In junior high school I continued to be very friend-focused, trying to fit into some sort of group in my borderline introverted way. Bobbi, just a few years behind me, came in and created her own social circles. She was, and always has been a beautiful and outgoing person. She ran with the popular crowd and always had boys vying for her attention. My bothersome little sister was *popular* and getting all the attention. How annoying!

By high school, I think we had a little competitive thing going on. She was *over* the charmingly sweet sister thing because I would not reciprocate. She ran with her friends and had a few parties where the whole high school and two more would show up. During one party in particular, my little brother Brian ended up calling the police to break it up. I wanted no part of that and hung out with my close-knit pack. I don't want to give the impression that we were adversaries, however, she did tell me once that *"I had no style,"* and she stole the heart of one boy I liked. We did spend time together and did sisterly things, but I didn't perceive or treat her as a friend. When I moved away for college, there were no tears shed.

I believe in our case that distance did make our hearts grow fonder. After months and then years of separation, we found a new appreciation for each other. Almost overnight, our sisterly bond became stronger than ever before. Being raised together by default, we had established a few strong elements of Tribe. We had years of sharing time and space that established common history. Since birth, we had seen each other's best and worst sides and knew each other's struggles and pains. We didn't have to *go there* with vulnerability because we *were* there. All we had to add was some enthusiasm, which was the fun part!

My charmingly sweet sister is back in my life, and we hug often. Bobbi is my deepest, truest friendship, and I feel solidity in who I am because of her. She is the first to sign up for my escapades and always has my back. We have raised our families together as next door neighbors, and it has been a joy. Of course, Bobbi is a founding member of my Tribe and my wing-gal on all of our GNO (Girls Night Out) retreats and social events.

I know how lucky I am to have a sister. There is no other relationship quite like it. We share every element of Tribe and are blessed to be connected by DNA and a lifetime of knowing. BFLT = best friends for a lifetime.

The Leaves that Grow to Flourish

The life you build for yourself is represented by the beautiful, thriving leaves in your tree of life. With the growth from the imperfectly perfect seed and soil of your external environment, you are provided with a strong foundation. Although unseen, your roots grow deep and wide, almost mirroring the branches above, keeping you grounded. The strength and support of your friendships are the trunk and branches that lift you up, always reaching higher year after year so that you can flourish.

Some seasons are better than others. Life brings its challenges. Sometimes our tree experiences ice storms, droughts, torrential winds, and even infestations. However, life is good and repeatedly offers growth and expansion opportunities. Your leaves are the product of the tree of life you, your family, and your Tribe have nurtured.

CHAPTER 3:

Friends—the Good, the Fad, and the Ugly

WHEN IT COMES to friends, there are several distinct relationship types. Because we are discussing what it means to be a friend and have meaningful friendships, it is important to know what you *want*—and what you do *not* want.

The following will distinguish and acknowledge the Good, the Fad, and the Ugly when it comes to friendships. After identifying the types of friends that you should approach with discretion, we will focus heavily on what we want because as the law of attraction dictates, what you focus on expands. Life enhancing relationships are worth our time and attention. Let's start by getting clear on what a friend is and what it is not.

Friends

The word *friend* is certainly a noun. Definitions vary but generally speaking characterized as a person one knows and has a bond of reciprocal sentiment, typically outside of family relations. The word friend is often used as a polite greeting for an acquaintance or even a stranger one comes upon.[14]

Most of us have many friends. We have neighbors that we wave to as we pass them on the street, so we consider them friends. Acquaintances that we bump into regularly at church or other social gatherings are friends. You may acknowledge a person who rides the same bus with a familiar hello or nod, thus considering them a friend. People you work with, go to school with, and members of society who you see at community events—all of these individuals, and many more, can be considered friends. Then to top it all off, many of us have hundreds, if not thousands, of social media friends. Many of our so-called friends are people we interact with on occasion in a generally positive way, however, we are often divested from their life and well-being.

This group of people is very important to our social wellness. They are the people in our different circles of life that see us, know us, and like us. These relationships give us a sense of belonging. Even though these relationships may never grow in depth, the recognition by friends tells us that we are valued and that we matter. Friends can be a great resource, and just because the relationships are mostly superficial does not mean that we do not need them. We do.

Now, let's bite the bullet and look at the wolf in sheep's clothing.

Frenemies

Frenemy is a metaphor and a blend of "friend" and "enemy" that refers to a person one is friendly to, yet one truly dislikes. This frenemy is kind to our face, however, unfavorable and sometimes even malicious behind our back.[15] Here are some ways this might show up:[16]

1. "Under the fictitious blanket of friendship one might experience backhanded complements or put-downs from this person.
2. She roots for you to do well just as long as it's not better than her.
3. She is jealous of you and almost everything about your life.
4. She pretends to be your friend yet has ulterior motives.

When I think of frenemies, I think of someone who is sweet and friendly to my face yet does not really care about me at all (other than what I can do for her). This person is a gossip behind your back and, if you pay attention, is probably sharing some unflattering things about other mutual friends *with you*.

Fortunately, you can turn up your radar and identify

frenemies before too much harm is done. Here are a few signs that your friend is really a frenemy:

1. She devalues your achievement and celebrates your setbacks. The only way she feels good about herself is to make others feel less than. She is jealous of your victories. She may offer lopsided compliments like, "Wow, you finally did it," or "Boy, you sure are lucky." When you fail, it makes her feel good by comparison.

2. Frenemies love gossiping. She loves talking behind your back, and she is more than happy to share any unkind things that have been said about you.

3. Inquiring minds want to know. A frenemy will ask you lots of questions, not because she cares about you, but rather to stock up ammunition for her next gossip session. A real friend would listen, offer good advice, and honestly tell you if she thought you were making a mistake. A frenemy's advice will be self-serving, and she will certainly allow you to make a mistake so that she feels better about herself.

4. She will playfully contribute passive aggressive remarks or actions. Playing it off as if she is joking, she may underhandedly compliment someone else, your opponent, to take a jab at you. A frenemy's compliments may be backhanded: "Your hair looks so much better now than that bleach blonde you used to have." She may also keep pertinent information from you or share misinformation to sabotage you.

If you discover you have a frenemy in the midst, some would suggest mirroring their behavior and giving it right back to them. As tempting as sweet revenge can be, energetically speaking, it will not be in your best interest to do so. As you progress through life, some frenemies will undoubtedly take notice. The more successful you become, the more you will attract envy and resentment from these individuals.

My best advice is to graciously distance yourself from any frenemies. By making yourself unavailable to her, she will have less and less ammunition and, eventually, get bored with you and find another target. You may be unable to do this because she may be a coworker or even worse, a family member. In this case, be aware of who she really is behind the deceptively friendly surface, and don't engage more than is required.

It makes me feel icky to even write about frenemies, they definitely fit into the "ugly" category. I believe as the years go by, we experience these individuals less often. Perhaps they are maturing and have learned to be better, outgrowing their unkind ways. The good news is that people are mostly good. Make a habit of paying attention to how people make you feel. Often your feelings will sense the truth, and you will discover those who are insincere. Also, your true friendships will not tolerate the frenemy's direct or indirect attacks on you or the Tribe.

Friendlies

When I was in college, my co-ed dorm girlfriends were what I call *friendlies*. I made this word up. Nonetheless, I strongly believe in friendlies. Have you ever invested in a relationship to the extent that it is important and meaningful to you, however, you discover one day that "she's just not that in-to-you," so to speak? Well if you have, you have been a victim of the "friendlies". You understand that it can be disappointing and, even painful, to learn that these women were not as good of friends as you originally thought.

In many situations, these relationships come about when you are connected by a period of time, an event, or some other communal interest. When I was in college, my co-ed friends tried to "protect me" by expressing concern that I was spending too much time with "the guys." Looking back, it was really just them looking out for themselves. It was not an act of friendship or loyalty but rather a selfish, offensive move to execute their own agenda. This was borderline frenemy behavior. However, the distinction was that they didn't in any way want to harm me; they just wanted my undivided attention.

Susan, a stay-at-home mom, provides another example. When she was a young mother, she tried to connect with other mothers through school activities for her children, in her own way "trying to fit in" at a new school. She was open and eager to build friendships and invested a lot of time, energy, and care into the kids, the school, and to these new *friends*. She and this group socialized regularly, attended all the kids' sporting events together, and even traveled together. Susan was going in deep, but the others had a different agenda. They were predominantly in it for convenience, not connection. After a few years, she finally figured it out. Susan was dismayed and hurt to recognize that they really didn't care about her at all beyond scheduling kids' playdates, class projects, and game time chitchat.

The *friendlies* are not to be a topic worthy of deep discussion, however, it is a distinction worth noting and comprehending. They fit in the "fad" category because to them, we are merely a temporary friendship fix. As we look back on our lives, we have to take responsibility for not recognizing the signs, or lack thereof, that friendlies won't evolve into friendship. Just like us, they were at different places in their own lives, and friendship wasn't on the agenda.

For a friend to become a friendship, there must be reciprocity. If you find yourself investing considerably more than another, recognize that your intentions don't line up, and move along. This may feel a bit like rejection, but it really isn't.

Friendship

I argue that friendship is not a noun as suggested by many dictionaries, but a verb.[17] Friendship requires action. A friend turns into a friendship when two people make a conscious decision to take the relationship to the next level. They make time to get to know each other one-on-one by doing things like scheduling a coffee date, going out to lunch, meeting up for a cocktail, or running together. Friendship requires an investment of time, attention, and enthusiasm. It is a process, a journey, and some would even say, an art. I would define friendship as the positive effort two individuals take to build a platonic relationship, establish common interests, and develop caring feelings for each other.

FRIENDSHIP = TIME + ATTENTION + ENTHUSIASM

It is so easy to add a friend to your roster. Why is it that we do not have more friendships? Well first and foremost, many people do not yet recognize the gap between friends and friendship. They can't imagine that friendship is lacking when they have hundreds of friends. Beyond that, the biggest obstacle most people face is that they don't make the time to invest in friendship. Let's face it, we are all busy. We have demanding jobs that take up at least half of our waking hours. Many of us have family responsibilities that can easily take up the other half! If you are a parent and still have kids at home, your child's social activities have likely trumped your own.

An American Time Use Survey in 2014 found that people ages 20–24 spent the most time per day socializing on average of any other age group.[18] In an article for *The Atlantic*, Professor Rawlins shared that the largest drop-off in friends occurs when people get married.[19] It seems odd that this would be the case since a wedding celebration usually brings all of your friends together to commemorate your union. It ends up being a farewell party of sorts for many of these friendships because the demands of married life are more pressing than friendship, and we simply forget to make the effort. Inadvertently, our new lives make us grow apart from our friendships.

Life Happens

Being a social person and compelled to be a connector, I can't say that was the case for me. After getting married,

I continued to organize gatherings for my expanded social circle. At least monthly, my girlfriends would get together for a game night called Bunco. After a year or so, we decided that we didn't need the game; we just really wanted to visit and drink wine together. So, that monthly event evolved into GNO (Girls Night Out). We planned an annual long weekend out-of-town getaway—a GNO Retreat.

My husband and I made our joint social lives a priority as well. We joined an adult co-ed softball team, where I served as captain (which really only meant that I did the legwork to build the team and get us signed up). The whole gang, often 10–15 guys and girls, would get together regularly at our house or a local pub after the games. We had some great times.

My husband, Parker, and I both wanted kids. But, for the first five years of our marriage, we were a little self-absorbed with our careers and having fun with our friends. Each year we would have a conversation and agree to wait to start our family. One night after a softball game, we had an aha moment—something was missing in our lives. That is when we decided we were ready to start trying to have a baby. We were blessed with a pregnancy within a few short months of that decision.

Uncharted Territory and Unintended Disconnection

The social events went uninterrupted for a time . . . until the scariest night of my life: August 28, 1999. Shook to the core and forever changed, this was the beginning of the end of my own social life. It was at this pivotal moment, that although my girlfriends were there for me and I loved them dearly, I shifted all of my attention away and began to lose that part of my soul.

It was a Saturday night, and I was 36 weeks pregnant. We went to bed like any other evening, however, a few hours into our slumber, I woke abruptly to find that my water had broken. Excited and anxious, I woke Parker, and we prepared to leave.

As I pulled my things together, I noticed something odd. The umbilical cord—the lifeline that provided my baby nourishment and oxygen—was way out of place. We rushed to the hospital. The ER staff hurried me in from the darkness to a bright fluorescent lit room, laid me on a gurney, and placed a fetal monitor on my belly. I distinctly heard a nurse mutter under her breath "*DEAD*...................."

The next thing I remember, I woke in a hospital room with a nurse holding my hand and no baby in sight. I cried out, "Is he ALIVE?!" The nurse exclaimed "YES! And he is doing wonderfully!" At birth, he was not breathing and had no heartbeat. The doctor and nurses resuscitated him. Later a nurse shared that these are the emergency situations that they train for.... . . but they usually don't turn out well. They called him their Miracle Baby.

People tell you your life is going to change when you have children. After this terrifying near-death experience, I literally left that hospital a different person. I know that the birth of one's first child is a momentous occasion for everyone, and we are all sure to have some trepidation. Despite that, I do feel like I suffered PTSD (post-traumatic stress disorder) for a few months, fearing the worst after such an agonizing experience.

Now, my mission and sole purpose was to keep this baby alive and nurture him to thrive.

Upon returning home, it was as if I now wore blinders. My single focused was this baby and my new role and title: mother. Abruptly and without intention, I offered little time or attention to my girlfriends. My neglect over the next eight years slowly created an empty space in my soul.

Women are fundamentally changed when a child enters their world. Add a traumatic event, and that single-mindedness may be intensified. Naturally, our lives will never be the same when we are blessed with a growing family to care for. It is at this time when many women begin what can be a decade's long process of letting themselves go. No time for personal recreation, interests and friendships. Nothing beyond the superficial anyway. We become lost; our soul resides just below that surface and is no longer fully nourished. We begin to feel something is missing, yet we don't understand why.

This is exactly what happened to me.

The Baby!

Of course, everyone and their grandmother came to meet the new baby, so our social lives did not tone down for some time. However, it did look quite different. Everything revolved around the baby. Baptisms, birthdays, and all *firsts* were celebrated. Even when the baby couldn't move around on his own, play dates were scheduled.

Even as a connector, I fell into the trap of not spending enough quality time with my close friends. What was once weekly get-togethers became monthly, yearly, or neglected completely. My girlfriend monthly GNO events continued for a few years . . . kind of. Our annual retreats ended abruptly a couple of years later after the birth of our daughter . . . mostly because I just didn't make them happen. For the next six years, I was almost exclusively focused on my family, and my friendships suffered. Social experts say this is somewhat natural. I think I could have done better. I have to give complete credit to one faithful member of my Tribe, who continued to put in the connecting effort even when I was self-centered and inattentive to our friendship.

We are all reading this book from different perspectives. Life is going to happen to us all throughout our presumably very long, fulfilling lives. When things are going great, it may be easier to focus on friendships. When things are challenging, sometimes our friendship efforts unwittingly get derailed. This is when we need these relationships the most. Friendships are the family you choose. They are unique and not bound by contract, duty, or responsibility. Without the formal family structure, friendships are vulnerable to neglect during stressful, busy times. As fragile as it may be, this weakness is also its strength because friendship is flexible. A relationship that has been invested in over time can survive bouts of neglect. A successful friendship prevails with no strings attached—except those you choose to tie.[20]

Friendships Fill Empty Spaces

Kyler Shumway, author of *The Friendship Formula* suggests that there are five essential food groups of friendship:[21]

1. *Companionship*—Whether going to an event together, eating out, going to a movie, taking a walk, or just hanging out, we enjoy other people's company and feel less awkward in social situations when we are not alone.

2. *Fun*—Shared interests and activities add to the positivity bank account and create fun memories. Enjoying a good laugh or an exhilarating experience together is priceless.

3. *Empathy*—Isn't it nice to be able to confide in someone and feel like you are heard and really seen? Just having someone who understands what we are going through is comforting. Empathy is the greatest of all human superpowers.

4. *Assistance*—Sometimes we just need a ride home from the mechanic. Maybe we need a hand moving something or help with a computer problem. Friendships can lend a hand when we are in a bind.

5. *Learning*—We all have special gifts and areas of expertise that can benefit others. Sharing these gifts with each other is rewarding and allows us to sharpen our own skills while teaching our friends something that will help them be successful. We can also learn together through life experience. The friendship journey is sure to have challenges. We can support each other, work through obstacles together, and learn as we go.

Tribal Friendships Open Hidden Places

Women have a sixth sense when it comes to communicating with each other. It really is a superpower. We *get* how the female brain works. We see things differently, and our feelings and responses to certain situations may seem *crazy* or just *weird* to the opposite sex. Your closest girlfriends likely *get you* in ways that even your spouse never will. Not only will they likely understand, but they will also back you up and validate your reasoning.

Women are natural born nurturers. We can openly share from the heart with our girlfriends without fear of judgment and can expect to be comforted. There is no shame in sharing our insecurities or discussing embarrassing topics. We can be totally open. Our big crazy dreams won't get squished but instead encouraged by these loving friends.

Some of you are already experiencing this security blanket of love and acceptance from one or more solid friendships. Some of you may need some help making this happen. In the chapters ahead we are going to break down each component of Tribal friendships. You will learn how to attract, build, and fortify your Tribe. One day soon, you will experience the joy and fulfilment of a Tribe that contributes to your own personal wholeness.

CHAPTER 4:

The Tribe

TRADITIONALLY, A TRIBE is a social division in society consisting of families or communities linked by social, economic, religious, or blood ties. Some Tribes have a common culture and dialect, and typically they have a recognized leader. A customary Tribe is a face-to-face community, relatively bound by kinship relations, reciprocal exchange, and strong ties to place.[22]

As my friend Michelle so eloquently outlined in the forward, the term Tribe should be utilized only with great respect and consideration of its origins. It is with the term's heritage in mind that I aspire to create that culture with my closest friends. This social division, group, or pack are linked by common social patterns, interests, and sometimes, goals. As the group connects together over time, they establish the Tribe's personality, lingo, patterns, and rituals. Outsiders that socialize with these lasting friends may get annoyed because of the inside jokes and private references. This culture may not be understood by others looking in, but the members find their intimacy endearing. They are tuned in to each other and get it!

It is important to differentiate a Tribe from a clique. No matter one's age, cliques can be a problem, especially for women. "Lady and the Tribe" in no way encourages exclusivity, snubbing or rudeness. This is the family YOU choose. Members are not voted on, and there is no election for a leader. A Tribe is not a clique or faction of exclusivity. By design, our Tribes have overlap and extension that breed's inclusivity.

The bond with your Tribe requires regular face-to-face contact. This regular contact creates a sense of belonging, enhancing the time and space (vicinity) of friendship. To super-simplify the formula:

TRIBE = FRIENDSHIP (TIME + ATTENTION + ENTHUSIASM) + SPACE + VULNERABILITY

Amanda Fewell, Transformational Speaker and Coach says "I notice such a difference in the vibe of a group depending on how many of us have been able to hang out one-on-one. Those one-on-one connections are essential to building the group dynamic. It's fun and juicy to be together. When there have been several individual connections going on, it almost feels like you get to have many connections at once. But if there hasn't been as much personal intimacy lately, it feels a little different—more general and diffused."[23]

Your Tribal place feels like home when you arrive. It is safe, encouraging and makes you feel relevant because you are truly seen. Your Tribe cares about your opinions and what you have to say. They are proud of your talents and strengths and are not threatened by your success. Your Tribe will promote rather than ignore or diminish your wins. Although these close friends can be a great influence for you to be better and do better, there is no contest; you do not feel competitive with one another. The experience of finding your Tribe can be life changing. It becomes a mirror reaffirming who you are and where you belong.

SOUL SISTERS—FRIENDS WHO GO THE DISTANCE

HOW DID YOU MEET?

Ruthie:
(Matter of fact) "We met at an SBA networking event, but we didn't really get to know each other until I randomly asked you to go to Durango with me."

Rachel:
(Aghast) "Nooo-ewww. We were friends before THAT! We went to Vegas before that!"

Ruthie:

(In protest) "No, we didn't! We talked and were friendly before that but . . ."

Rachel:

(Laughing) "No, you are completely wrong."

Ruthie:

(Perplexed) "Maybe I am wrong? When did we go to Vegas? Was that even you?" (Laughing)

Rachel:

(Bursts out laughing)

Ten years ago, the Durango trip was when Ruthie and Rachel really started going deep and sharing their lives. They went to visit Ruthie's daughter in college. Ruthie invited Rachel to go, and she thought, "why not?"

Rachel:

"It was kind of weird. You just don't usually invite someone to visit your daughter in college."

Ruthie:

"Yes, it was really random. We didn't even turn the radio on. It was when I was starting to go through some things, and I needed someone who didn't know and wouldn't judge all of my baggage."

The two really got to know each other on that road trip.

Rachel:

"When you have time like that, you can really get into each other's brain and see how they think."

Today, Ruthie is a flight attendant, and her career has her traveling 75% of the year.

Ruthie:

"Ours is nice because it's not a friendship that you have to worry about maintaining. It doesn't matter what I am going through or she is going through, we listen to each other. She knows I would drop everything to come to help her if she needed it, but if she doesn't hear from me for a while, she isn't going to get mad."

Ruthie and Rachel both have recalled relationships with other women who got upset if they dropped off the face of the earth for a while and didn't connect.

Rachel:

"We both have a tendency to do that, so we aren't bothered by it. If I forget her birthday and three months later say, 'Hey, happy belated birthday,' she would be cool with that."

Ruthie:

Rachel can tell when I am stressed out, even when posting on Facebook. It's funny because no one else can tell, but she will read between the lines and drop me an email or text saying, 'Hey, are you ok?' when no one else will pick up on it."

Ruthie (addressing Rachel, choked up):

"I think I'm going to cry. That's why I think of you as my best friend. You do listen; you don't judge; and you don't give unsolicited advice. Everyone else seems to add to my anxiety, telling me what I should or shouldn't do instead of giving me the tools to do it—or just listen."

Rachel:

"Most of the time you have a judge-y friend . . . or a good listener who wants to solve all of your problems. All I want is someone to listen and say, 'You will be fine, you've got this.'"

Ruthie:

"Another thing I notice about our friendship is that, when we go out, we don't reminisce about the past, and instead we talk about the future."

Rachel:

"Ah . . . yeah . . . I don't remember . . . maybe that's why."

(They both burst out laughing)

Ruthie:

"That is why I love you, (still laughing), some things we don't need to be reminded of."

Rachel:

"Early on, you created a persona and wall around yourself, and I very much wanted to get behind that wall because I knew that was not who you really were. Once I got behind that wall, I thought, 'I like this Ruthie.' My job is to constantly reiterate how awesome Ruthie is, so when she puts that wall up . . . I remind her.

(Looking at Ruthie) "It's okay if you put it up for everyone else, but don't put that wall up for me because I love the Ruthie that is on the inside of the wall."

Ruthie:

"Yes, back then I felt like I was hiding in public because I put myself out there in a big way, but it was not who I really was. I was always told who I was, but I didn't really know myself. When you aren't happy with who you are, you cling to whatever security you can find. I was in a 30-year marriage; I became the person I thought he wanted. I became a prostitute of sorts 'Who can I be for you . . . and you . . . and you?' The reason I think of you as my best friend, Rachel, is that looking back, I think I was emotionally abused."

Rachel:
"Oh yeah. For sure. I think I am the only one who honed in on it and was vocal with you about it."

Ruthie:
"My other friends didn't see it—or didn't want to see it. When I decided to leave my husband, I told a handful of people what I wanted to do. A few of them told me I shouldn't do it, but Rachel encouraged me and gave me strength."

Ruthie reaches across the table and grabs Rachel's hand. With tears in her eyes and voice trembling, she says, "Rachel, you really do give me strength. I don't think I could have done it without you."

Rachel:
(Moved and also choked up) "Awe . . . that's so sweet!"

Ruthie:

"I am usually hundreds, if not thousands, of miles away, but I am always just a plane ride away. The distance is actually good. We can weigh in on ideas and problems only invested in our friend's best interest."

"I have one or two other very good friends. But core, deep down inside, it's Rachel. It will always be Rachel. (Ruthie looks at Rachel) It will always be you; you are my bestest friend. You are my deepest friendship, Rachel."

(Holding hands again)

Rachel:

(Touched) "Oh you are mine too!"

WHAT IS YOUR ADVICE TO WOMEN WHO DON'T FEEL LIKE THEY HAVE A DEEP FRIENDSHIP OR BEST FRIEND?

Ruthie:

"Take the risk and ask if they would like to go to Durango" (she chuckles). Rachel came into my life when I had no best friends. Well, actually, my best friend was beating me up, and my other best friend I felt was using me. I couldn't talk to them about anything. Find that one person who shows you that they have two ears and one mouth and will really listen."

Rachel:

"Find someone who enjoys listening to you. Don't be afraid to share really personal things for fear of damaging a perfect image. The people I am closest with are constantly sharing their struggles, not just their successes."

Long-Distance Friendships

Just a quick note about long-distance friends. If you have long-distance friendships, let me say that I commend you! It's not easy to maintain a strong long-distance friendship. In this book, we are focusing primarily on in-person relationships because they allow you to grow and become fulfilled through regular interactions. Although your long-distance friends may not be part of your in-person Tribe on a regular basis, they can still participate in your life in a meaningful way. I consider these individuals our soul sisters or our Tribe once removed. We are connected for a lifetime but on different paths. We may not be able to see each other regularly, but when we do, we haven't skipped a beat. The great news is that we can have both an in-person Tribe and dear friends who are far away. When long-distance friends come to town, they too can join the Tribe's activities! If you have moved and feel like you are starting over, fear not! You can cultivate new in-person friendships, build a Tribe, and still maintain your long-distance friendships.

Guy Friendships versus Girl Friendships

I remember a time when I had more guy friends than girl-friends. Now I am not talking about boyfriends here, so make no mistake. It was when I moved away from home and was solo for the first time. Well, maybe *dropped off* is a more accurate description. I was enrolled to attend a college that was 400 miles from my hometown and far away from the friends I had managed to develop over the previous five years. I was sad but also excited for the adventure ahead. My experience of starting over and being the new kid when I was growing up was about to pay off—I was fearless and ready.

This time, however, I was not alone. Everyone at freshman orientation was also experiencing a new environment. We all were starting with a clean slate, socially speaking. My assigned roommate was a granola from Aspen, Colorado, and my suitemates were foreign exchange students from Japan. The dorm I selected was co-ed, however, each suite was divided by gender. I immediately began testing the waters of friendship to see where I fit in. Who were my people? As you might expect, I started off with the girls on my floor and then expanded the search within my classrooms.

Everything was going pretty well. I was connecting and having fun with these new people. I met my first love interest in softball, a physical education class. After a few months of flirting and hanging out, we officially started dating. It was at this time that I started spending more time with the boyfriend and had less time to hang out with the new friends I had made. I remember one friend in particular who had assumed a *motherly* demeanor in the dorm. She confronted me and shared her concern that I was spending too much time with *this guy*. Well, young love will not be hindered by the jealous whims of a few catty *friendlies*. Her proclamation sent me further and faster into the company of the boyfriend and his fellas.

These guys were fun. Always kidding around, doing goofy and dumb things. They often playfully challenged each other to friendly competition and bonded over Coors Light. It was highly entertaining to witness. I, the token female, was included with a friendly tease here and there and made to feel like part of their pack. There was no drama, pettiness, or catfighting. They interacted with ease and cohesiveness yet were quite independent of each other. The relationships were simple and easy.

I did create a few friendships with girls during my co-ed years, but now looking back, I can't say that I am still connected to any of them. The relationships did not have enough history to sustain them. Back then, I was *in love* and wasn't feeling any need for other deep connections and girlfriends. It wasn't until we got married six years later and moved back home, closer to old friends and family, that I realized I was missing the support of other women in my life.

Men and women are just different when it comes to their needs and expectations of friendship. When asked to define friendship in a British study, Marin Crawford found that men and women had completely different answers.[24] The results were incredibly consistent. Women shared about trust and confidentiality whereas men described a friend as someone to go out with or someone they enjoyed hanging out with. Men's friendships are based on activities, and women's are about sharing. A man will describe a very good friend as a guy he sees at the annual fantasy football draft or someone he recently met over a round of golf. But are they really friends? Not by a woman's standard.

Why are deep friendships so rare in men? Why is our definition so very different? Experts would say with certainty, its conditioning. In our society, with the exception of shaking hands, men are not even allowed to touch each other beyond a slap on the back. "Sexperts" Dick and Paula McDonald, authors of *Loving Free*, suggest that most men do not have role models nor practice in the art of intimacy with their fellow man. Little girls can hug, kiss and hold hands and cry. They can without fear say "You're my best friend, I love you." Little boys don't dare.[25]

Experts agree that most men do not have as many close friendships as would be beneficial to them. Few men have had the opportunity and upbringing to be open and vulnerable in a relationship, and they are simply not aware of this immense void in their emotional lives. They haven't got a clue of what they are missing. This saddens me deeply. However, because we are so different, and my passion is for girl Tribes, this book is written for women. Maybe there will be a He-Tribe sequel!

Generally speaking, women long for more primitive patterns of social connection, interdependence and cohesion. We are better at reading nuances in other's reactions and behavior. Women are just more interested in relationships. This is even evident in newborn babies before social conditioning could have any effect. Baby girls that are even just hours old are more attracted to faces. Baby boys are more attracted to shapes and patterns. Additionally, baby girls maintain eye contact two to three times longer than baby boys.[26] Females just bond. We don't need sports, nicknames, or funny handshakes. All we need for bonding is a couple of comfy chairs and a pot of tea.

Jenny

I just love the name Jenny. When I hear it, I immediately feel love, warmth, and a sense of comfort. My Tribe story begins here. I met Jenny shortly after moving to a new junior high school, second quarter of seventh grade. I was shy but eager to make new friends.

As I was off to another fresh start in a new school, this time I was lucky because I had one friend already. Her name was Debbie. Debbie had become a friend because our parents were friends first. We would get to hang out when our folks socialized. When I moved to her school, Debbie graciously introduced me to all of her friends, what I would later refer to as "the group." Jenny and Debbie had been friends since grade school, and now Jenny was my friend too.

Jenny was welcoming and easy to get to know. We shared a few classes. I remember bonding in the alto section during choir most of all. It didn't take long before we were inseparable. We rode our bikes to parks, the local swimming pool, and all over town. We enjoyed sleepovers and doing Jane Fonda's exercise videos. We would hang out with her dog, Pierre, and our friend, Tom, on her front porch for hours. She had a real jukebox in her basement with the best music: Foreigner 4, Journey, Loverboy, Air Supply, Night Ranger—you name it! We would lay out in my backyard covered in baby oil and listen to the radio while trying to quickly press "record" on a cassette tape to capture our favorite songs. We would take a dip in my parent's hot tub and had our first *adult* drink together—beer with Kool-Aid (we didn't care for the beer by itself).

One summer we spent countless hours watching and re-watching movies. We loved scary movies like *The Changeling, Friday the 13th, and Halloween.* Our favorite movie that summer was *Grease 2.* Historically viewed as a theatrical flop . . . we loved it, watched it dozens of times, and memorized every scene and song. We could sing every lyric. I think we invented binge watching back in 1985.

We continued to be best friends into high school, and at the age of 15, we shared our first job at Grandpa's Burger Haven, a local greasy spoon that boasted an eight-inch wide hamburger. Together, we moved on to another, more popular chain restaurant, where we spent three years in polyester uniforms learning everything there was to know about fast food for $3.35 per hour. One morning I went to work, and my fingers were adorned with a bright set of press-on nails. I was charged with mixing up the biscuit dough and baking them for the breakfast sandwich assembly line. An hour or so into my baking, much to my dismay, I noticed that I had lost a few of my fake nails as I kneaded the dough. I shared my surprise with Jenny who had been working the biscuit sandwich line. She had found them . . . and removed them . . . before sending the biscuit sandwich off. We were 16, we laughed, and it seemed okay to both of us at the time.

We both bought our first car when we turned 16. I had a 1978 Chevy Chevette, and Jenny had a 1977 Ford Mustang. Cruising Main Street in Longmont, Colorado, was a popular pastime. The three local high schools and others would come together for this Friday and Saturday night ritual. Main Street is a 22-block straight stretch right down the middle of Longmont. Young adults from Wyoming to Denver would travel here to "cruise the strip." We would drive back and forth for hours with our friends hanging out the windows and visiting with other cars going the same direction. It's no wonder Longmont outlawed cruising shortly after we graduated.

We were mostly on the straight and narrow but got into our share of trouble. We strategically chose the same jobs, classes, and hobbies but never the same boyfriends. Upon graduation, we were separated for a few years, but now as adults, we are reconnected with a bond as strong as ever. Our mothers and daughters also became great friends. Jenny holds the title, and always will as my longest, dearest BFF. I love the name Jenny. Jenny feels like home.

Over the years I have known dozens of women who have developed their own Tribes. Although most didn't set out with the concept of a Tribe in mind, they did bond with their friends intentionally. They make relationships a priority and carve out time for one another. They check-in on a regular basis, scheduling dates for lunch, shopping, or a glass of wine. Some women facilitate a Girls Night Out each month. There are no rules here other than the required Tribal formula:

TRIBE = FRIENDSHIP + SPACE + VULNERABILITY

On a personal note, my investment in friendships has established one of the most rewarding segments of my life—one that honors my soul, fills me with joy, and provides me with purpose. Even Jesus chose to spend much of his time in small groups, building deep relationships with a few significant people rather than speaking to large crowds. As a species, we were created to live in small, strong, close-knit Tribes or communities. Our need for social connection and Tribal instinct is a deep-rooted part of human nature, programmed into the human brain by our own evolution. Perhaps life has detoured you from connecting on a meaningful level, or maybe you are already well on your way to Tribal bliss. No matter where you are with your inner circle, I am certain that together, we can find, build, and fortify your very own Tribe.

CHAPTER 5:

The Leader of
Your Tribe

IF YOU ALREADY have a few friends who have the potential to become your Tribe, you may be wondering, who is going to be the leader? If I am starting fresh, what kind of person will lead us?

Tribes are about faith in each other and belief in the idea of this elite community. Who is going to inspire this Tribe and create its own heart and soul that is bigger than any one of us alone? Who will have the strength, perseverance, and direction to bond us together? Well the answer, my friend, is—that leader is you.

You are the leader of your Tribe. Don't let that stress you out. Although a very important role, you already have everything you need. Your Tribe only needs three things:

- Common interests
- Communication
- Bonding moments

Common Interests

What common interests do you share with your best friends? Are you all super achievers, professional powerhouses in your respective fields? Do you love to travel? Are you all mothers at different stages of raising your family? Maybe you will have a wide variety of these individuals in your Tribe.

In my Tribe, we share interests such as:

- The law of attraction
- Striving to be our best through diet, exercise, and personal development
- Our children
- Travel
- Self-care
- Common interests
- Spirituality
- A quest to feel whole
- Our friendships

Your Tribe will have different interests that connect you.

As you are thinking about who may be a good fit, common interests are a good place to start.

Communication

Regular communication is key and gives a Tribe its mojo. Intentionally connecting weekly by reaching out with a phone call or even just a "thinking of you" text fills the friendship's positivity tank. I believe strongly that Tribes should connect face-to-face at least once a month. Video chat is better than nothing, but preferably, plan to meet in person so you can exchange hugs and squeezes. There is nothing that can replace the physical touch we need. According to Healthline, the part of each woman's brain associated with stress showed reduced activity after a hug. Hugging also increased activity in the part of the brain associated with maternal behavior. [27]

Bonding Moments

Bonding moments can just naturally happen, however, having a plan or routine in place to strengthen these relationships is a very good idea. After my six-year hiatus I was feeling empty, and it was time to "get the band back together" so to speak. Since then, with the exception of some required *social distancing*, we have gathered almost every month and have not missed one retreat. We have reserved the third Thursday of each month for "Women Who Wine," a two-hour happy hour at one of our homes. We guard and protect this special time together because it reconnects us and keeps us tuned in to each other's lives. Our annual retreat is a three-night getaway filled to the brim with bonding moments. This is set up months in advance, so we can eagerly plan and have something to look forward to. The weekend is sacred to who we are, held in high regard and coveted by the Tribe's members.

Leading Your Tribe

Leading your Tribe starts with a decision to make your friendships a priority. Next, it takes some intention. The objective is to create your Tribe's culture. What do you want it to be? How will it make the lives of its members better? How will you protect it? The last thing it requires is a plan. If you just wait for things to happen, assuming they will happen organically, you risk that *life* will take over and sideline your Tribe. Don't let that six-year gap happen to you. Take the lead and invest in your Tribe.

The truth is that each of us is the leader of our own Tribe. Just like marriage requires more than a 50/50 split in effort, Tribal fellowships thrive at a 100/100 commitment from its members. Each leader within your Tribe has something to give and should want to add value. An individual's strengths will dictate how they will contribute as a leader to the Tribe. One gal may be the best at knowing when to reach out with a phone call just when it's needed. Another makes herself available to show up for you when you need support. Someone else may be great at organizing events, and another Tribe-mate may have skills at building on that bonding time with activities. Everyone has a role to play, everyone leads the Tribe.

No Two Tribes Look Alike

Just because I have picked out my three to six besties does not mean they share the same connections with each other. By design, our Tribes are inclusive with friendship overlap and extension. Each member may have her own unique group she considers her Tribe. Additionally, we will all certainly have multiple friendship circles that extend beyond our Tribe. These are friendship groups that fit within a specific part of our life. They could include work friends, tennis buddies, or a mom's group. Some of these special friendships may individually become a best friend and member of your Tribe. These ladies are special to you, adding value in immeasurable ways. Your Tribe is the hub of your network of relationships that make up its own community, what I will call our Kindred Clan.

A Martyr Makes a Poor Leader

Now that we have established that only YOU can lead your Tribe, the first thing to remember is that the best leaders practice self-care. The tendency "to always put yourself last" has to go! When you continually take care of everyone and everything but yourself, you gradually have less and less to give. If you don't KILL the martyr within you, you unknowingly will become needy. We all know that person who unknowingly has become an energy vampire because they don't make themselves a priority. The impact is exactly opposite of what they intend since they don't have anything left and need others in a disproportionate way to fill them up. Don't be that vamp! Take care of yourself so that you know who you are and what you bring to the table. At your best, you are a Rock Star! Find her.

Reconnecting to who you really are is easier than you think. It requires self-care, self-love, and getting your needs met. What do you need? What would fill you up and make you feel better? Maybe you've gone so far down the path of service that you can't even answer this right now. If this is the case, carving out a little ME time is important. Take time to sit and be quiet with yourself and the universe and remember what lights your fire. Think about a time in your life when you were eager and excited. What is it you were doing? Who were you with? Why was it so special? What activities made you joyful? Was it singing, dancing, painting, or writing? Are you doing these things now? You need to! Doctor's orders! This fills your tank, so you have more to give . . . which you also love. You are a giver.

Once you know what you need, all you have to do is ASK for it! Guess what? Your friends and family can't read your mind. They don't know what you need and can't help if they don't understand. Believe it or not, other people also like to be of service! YOU need to be #1 in your own life! Drop the guilt trip! Once you do this and become a leader in your own life, you will be WHOLE. Everyone around you benefits when you are whole.

All too often we diminish our talents, skills, and abilities so as not to seem boastful when what we should be doing is fully sharing our God-given gifts with others. We fear that our strengths will make others feel weak, our knowledge will make others feel foolish, and our triumphs will make others feel unsuccessful. Nothing could be further from the truth. No one benefits from you playing small. Sharing your gifts raises everyone up and encourages them to do the same. We want to see the whole you in all of God's glory—just as you want to see others in theirs.[28]

We all must regularly remind ourselves that our gifts are meant to be shared. Leading with our talents is not boastful. The promise to do our best with this God-given opportunity to expand life is fulfilling. In doing so, we can be of service to others.

Are we on the same page now? Can we agree that you are the leader of your Tribe, and the first order of business is to fill your own tank? You may not feel you are leadership material, but if you don't advocate for and lead yourself, you will not have the fuel to be much more than a passenger in life. Be #1 in your own life.

KNOWING YOU

The greatest wisdom one can possess is discovering who you are. Recognize who and what you love and what your goals, morals, needs, and standards are. Knowing what you live for, what you will not tolerate, and what you are willing to die for defines who you are.[29].

Let's take a few moments to ask ourselves these questions. Get a pen right now and write your short answers for yourself.

This is just meant to be a quick brainstorming session. Jot your answers here (~3–5 responses for each).

MY GOALS:

1.

2.

3.

4.

5.

WHAT I LOVE:

1.

2.

3.

4.

5.

MY KEY BELIEFS—WHAT IS "RIGHT"?

1.

2.

3.

4.

5.

WHAT FILLS MY TANK? WHAT INTERESTS AND ACTIVITIES DO I NEED TO FEEL WHOLE?

1.

2.

3.

4.

5.

WHAT PERSONAL STANDARDS
DO I HAVE FOR MYSELF?

1.

2.

3.

4.

5.

WHAT OR WHO AM I SO IMPASSIONED
ABOUT THAT I RELENTLESSLY PURSUE ITS/
THEIR SUCCESS, EVEN TO MY OWN DEMISE?
(IN LIEU OF SELF-PRESERVATION LET'S
LIMIT THIS ANSWER TO ONE OR TWO.)

1.

2.

Well done! How does it feel to give life to the values that make you tick? Later in a separate notebook, sit with these answers one at a time and journal on each one of them. Give yourself the gift of this time to get to know yourself better. It may take only 15 minutes for each section, or it could take an hour or more.

There is power in putting ideas down on paper. Enjoy this creative exercise. Allow yourself to feel these answers and honor them with acceptance. This will give life to the elements of your being that have yet to be identified. What is going on in your mind, body, and spirit? Who are you?

Write in your journal:

1. For each goal, answer these questions:
   a. What inspires you to reach that target?
   b. What will it mean to you once you accomplish that objective?

2. Now write as if you have already reached the goal.
   a. How has the journey to your goal enhanced your life?
   b. How do you feel about yourself now that you have achieved the goal?
   c. How did your friends and family support you in this journey?
   d. How did you celebrate?

3. For each of your loves, try to put into words how this fondness makes you feel.
   a. What do you endear about this affection?
   b. How do you like to support this passion?
   c. What practices help you express this love?

4. Describe events or experiences that may have established your ethics.
   a. What ethical dilemmas have you faced?
   b. What makes a person act ethically or unethically?

5. List some of your interests and preferences.
   a. What activities and adventures fill you up and give you energy?
   b. What would your life be like if you made time to do one of these things every day?

6. Describe important standards that you live by.
   a. Is this something you were taught or is there a story behind this practice?
   b. Why are these principles so meaningful to you?

7. Explain for whom or what you will stand and defend at any cost.
   a. What makes you so passionate about this?
   b. Is there a story here?
   c. How do you support this desire?

Congratulations on completing this assignment! You now understand the energy of that exercise and likely can already feel it working for your benefit. Follow up by reading these answers to yourself every day until you really own who you are. Repeat the practice daily for 21–31 days. Each day, read aloud your goals and describe them as if you are already living the victory. Allow yourself to feel the accomplishment. This practice ignites the law of attraction. The Law of Attraction is our capability to attract what we want into our lives by giving it our focused attention.[30] Committing to this practice will provide you with affirming signs along your journey.

Remember, you are the leader of your Tribe. A Tribe has three simple elements: common interests, bonding moments, and communication. Becoming the leader of your own Tribe requires that you show up for yourself as a leader first in your own life. Don't expect to be *Superwoman*—everything for everyone all the time. You are pretty *Super* just the way God made you, and there is no need to constantly prove it to everyone else. Nobody is asking that of you, so give yourself a break! Make a practice of pampering yourself regularly. What are you going to do for yourself this week?

CHAPTER 6:

The Friendship Target

SO WHAT IS the magic number that makes a successful Tribe? How many friends and friendships beyond that
should we have? To begin with, let's talk about our capacity
for relationships.

Did you know that scientists have determined that there
is a finite number when it comes to relationships? Dr. Robin
Dunbar, in his studies in evolutionary anthropology, wanted
to know how many people the average person knows. Along
with other researchers, Dunbar determined that people are
connected in a variety of ways to about 150 others. This inves-
tigation of social patterns suggests that it really doesn't matter

how big your neighborhood is, how often you network, or if you are a social butterfly. Individuals seem to connect with no more than about 150 people.[31]

You may be plumping up with some pride here and thinking . . . "Oh boy, I am a super-achiever connector because I have 500, 1000, or 5000 friends on social media alone! I check in every day and connect to them all with a status update! I communicate with hundreds if not thousands of my followers each week." Many people believe that this is a super-efficient and effective way to maintain friendships. Although social media can certainly be helpful in reaching out and staying connected, it does not really contribute to the Friendship Formula:

FRIENDSHIP = TIME + ATTENTION + ENTHUSIASM

You will see and be seen by many of your friendships with social media. However, Dunbar points out that the 150 friends are relationships that you share personal history with, not those with whom you merely exchange small talk. For our purposes, we should expect our capacity for friendship to be about 150 and as we discussed earlier, there are many types of "friends."

How do you feel about that limit? Is the number too high or too low? To be quite honest, at first, I did not like this boundary. It seemed low to me, and I don't care for limits—especially when it comes to relationships. When I considered it further, I opened up to the concept since it was apparently scientifically proven. When I actually started thinking about the people with whom I spend time and attention, I settled in with acceptance. Dr. Dunbar defines a relationship as more than just names and faces. Rather, a relationship involves trust and obligation.[31]

There is nothing to say that one should set this as a relationship goal. Don't feel like you need to find and maintain 150 friendships to be happy. You will have other people who are included in this number that you may not even consider to be a friend. If you generally recognize them as being a part of your life, regardless of how you feel about them, they would be included.

Way back in about 340 BC Aristotle, a philosopher in Ancient Greece, had his own theory on friendship. He believed that a well-lived life must be built around companionship and that there were three types of friendships: utility, pleasure, and good. He would describe the first two types as *accidental* and the latter as *intentional*.[32]

Utility friendships are characterized as those serving the needs of the two parties.[33] They are not connecting for camaraderie or affection but rather "What's in it for me?" Each party receives a benefit of some sort in exchange. When the benefit ends, so does the relationship. Aristotle stated that utility friendships are more common in "older folks." I could not find an age range to share, so let's just call it adults.

Pleasure friendships, according to Aristotle, are based on . . . you guessed it . . . pleasure. He describes this one as more popular with "younger" people, such as college students or those who participate in sports. He explains that a pleasure friendship is more emotional and is often short-lived. It will continue as long as the two individuals gain enjoyment with an external mutual interest.

The majority of one's relationships may fall in the first two accidental friendships. Although Aristotle did not claim that these friendships were bad, he felt that the depth of the relationship limited its quality. It is important to have a few of the third type of friendship, which he identified as *good*.

Good friendships are based on mutual appreciation and the virtues they each hold dear. Who they are and what they represent encourage the two parties to connect and be regular participants in each other's lives. Aristotle said that, rather than being short-term, the *good* friendship often lasts until the end. In addition to depth and intimacy, the *good* include all the benefits of utility and beneficial friendships.

I can't say that I completely agree with Aristotle, but who am I to question a legend who has influenced astronomy, physics, ethics, and economics as we know it? I do appreciate that he found friendship an important enough topic to describe it as one of the true joys of life.

There are many layers of friendship, and we will expand on this concept. However, the following is still not a complete list as there are many gray areas between each layer in which a friend or friendship could lay. Here we will identify categories and descriptions for friendships that go beyond Aristotle's "types" and the types of friends that were introduced in chapter 3. It is called the Friendship Target, and it visually represents the layers of relationships that we might have. You will notice that family is not a layer in and of itself, because our family could possibly fit into any of the layers based on our connect-edness. Let's discuss each layer, working from the outside in, and how they fit into your social experience.

Your Community

When you think of a community, you may think about the place you live: your neighborhood, town, city, state, or even country. In respect to the Friendship Target, your community consists of friendships in the most casual sense of the word. In some ways, we are linked to them by the places we frequent, activities we enjoy, our mutual acquaintances, and our family routines. We see these people and recognize them in our shared context, and we are friendly with one another.

When it comes to community friendships, there is little expectation that we would know much about each other beyond the circumstance in which we connect. We may recognize and have a friendly conversation with a parent who has a daughter on the same team as ours, but our exposure is limited to the gym or ball field. We would probably learn something about someone's business if we network together, but we may not know a thing about their family. We may visit the same checker at the grocery store and exchange some niceties, chat about our plans for the 60 hot dogs we are buying, and share a chuckle. These are friends that we would not be likely to contact unless it was in regard to a common interest, organization, or activity.

This familiarity offers us a sense of support in various environments. These friends are resources to us and can offer information, recommendations, and help us make connections. Community members can come together for a cause and assist each other in reaching common goals. Our communities could consist of hundreds of people and may or may not be included in Dunbar's 150 friendship limit. Although not intimate in any way, our community is the first building block of the Tribe. Friendships throughout the Friendship Target all begin here.

The Friendlies

To refresh your memory, the *friendlies* are relationships that are somewhat superficial. Now I should digress a little here because I may have given the impression that these are *mean girls*, or superficial people. They are not. The *friendlies* friendship is not fake. It is real, and you can share great times together. The connection most of the time is authentic, but the relationship itself only touches on the superficial.

These can be quite enjoyable relationships, light and fun with a lot of laughter. You may end up spending quite a bit of time with the *friendlies* because they are convenient. These friends are probably in a similar place in life as you. Maybe you have children the same age, you have mutual friends, you work together, or you live in the same dorm. This convenience is what makes the friendship work.

However, once the convenience factor fades, these friendships usually falter. Like in Susan's example, this often happens to moms who get involved with their child's school activities. You may be making an investment of years with their class by connecting to students and parents alike. Unlike the soccer moms in your community, the *friendlies* moms share more consistency and more time together overall. You may spend hundreds of hours watching school sports together and hanging out afterward. Maybe you even go to dinner with the other families somewhat regularly. But, things can quickly change when kids transition to other schools, activities, and sports. The parents are most likely going to follow their kid's interests, and in effect, have little or no time for you or the pack they used to run with. When the built-in consistency with the *friendlies* gets disrupted, it cannot be sustained because there is no depth to the relationship.

The truth is that you absolutely want and need the *friendlies* in your Friendship Target. Most of the time they are simple, handy, and fun. The problem with this category is our own expectations.

Similar to Susan's story, I experienced a time when my closest friends weren't meeting up very often. We were all a little overwhelmed with parenthood, couplehood, or just adulting.

Building our own lives with new routines, stresses, careers, and kiddos, we had a lot on our plates. I for one was just trying to keep it all together and focusing on my kids: their education, their activities, and their social lives. Yes, I was THAT mom—guilty of making it all about my son and daughter. Of course, I also worked full time and did my best to keep up the household. With all this, who had time for a social life? It was easy to begin connecting with moms at the school. I liked these women, and I was open to building relationships with them. I misread our pleasant interactions and the fun we were having as real bonding. It was not. When life moved along and getting together became inconvenient, I was hurt that the others didn't make more of an effort to stay connected. I take responsibility for expecting more from those relationships that were opportune, superficial, and really all about our kids.

So recognize and take advantage of the *friendlies* for what they are: a pleasant way to pass time without requiring a big emotional investment. You likely share a common interest like your kids who, for both of you, have become your entertainment budget when it comes to discretionary income and time. You are there to watch a game, see a play, tour a science fair, or help sell Girl Scout cookies. You are *not* there to build deep connections. At any given time, you may have a dozen or more *friendlies* in your life. Once your tour together is over, they will likely transition to the community sector of your Friendship Target.

Your Kindred Clan

The next level of the Friendship Target is the Kindred Clan. Earlier we discussed the notion that no two Tribes are alike. My three to five BFFs may not share the same relationship with each other. For example, my sister, Bobbi, is most certainly a member of my Tribe and one of my five BFF's. However, Bobbi's Tribe includes Katherine and Aparna. I get to enjoy hanging out with Kathrine and Aparna on occasion since I am a member of Bobbi's Tribe. Our Tribes share members and then extend beyond reaching a sisterhood that becomes our Kindred Clan. When we socialize together as a group (for example, at our monthly Women Who Wine happy hour), we mesh all of our Tribes and build this network of high-level friendships.

This is the group of women you socialize with on a somewhat regular basis, perhaps monthly. These are the ladies that we love keeping up with, and a few hours here and there is just enough to keep the connection solid. This group makes us feel socially grounded, rooted, and intertwined. A Kindred Clan may boast dozens of women, or an intimate seven to twelve. They are invited to our milestones and special occasions, as we are to theirs. Together we share joyful times, witness accomplishments, and cheer for each other in moments of victory. Our Kindred Clan is a space where our Tribes meet.

LORI

Cousin Lori is definitely part of my Kindred Clan. Growing up, we got to see each other just once or twice a year since she lived in Kansas, and we were *somewhere* in northern Colorado.

My mom's siblings would celebrate a late Christmas together, rotating hosts each year. This event was a two- to three-day whirlwind of meals, activities and just spending time together. It was not about gifts, although the adults did draw names for the kids to keep us interested. My seven cousins along with my sister, brother, and I would quickly get reacquainted and begin planning our Christmas pageant, a tradition we started all on our own. It was a variety show we crafted, with the ten of us as the stars of the show. The adults would obediently watch with interest, and dear Aunt Ina would ooh and ahh at the depths of our talent and creativity. Because of the hundreds of miles that separated us, for the most part, we only got to see my mom's side of the family at Christmas. My mom and her sister Miriam (Lori's mom) were pretty close and we spent a few family vacations together.

Since we have all grown up and started families of our own, it has been much harder to stay connected. We do not get to see the Kansas clan even once a year, however, we are working on ways to start the annual celebration up again.

Cousin Lori is an amazing woman. She is super smart and has incredible business savvy. We took a family trip to Europe to visit Lori, who was studying abroad in Germany at the time. She graduated and earned a high-profile position with a big marketing company in Chicago where she thrived. Years later she got married and moved back to the farm in Kansas to raise her family. She started her own marketing agency and leads many projects for high-profile companies. On top of all that she, almost single-handedly, has kept the connections current with her Colorado cousins. Lori brings her family to visit us almost every year. She comes out in the fall for our GNO women's retreat, where she is *everyone's* cousin Lori. I am grateful for the fact that Lori has made this effort on a regular basis and I get to include her as a member of my Kindred Clan.

Your Soul Sisters

We all have important friendships that we don't have access to on a regular basis. These women would most likely be Tribal members if they were not separated from us by time and space. Often these friendships once enjoyed both proximity and regularity. We share history and fond memories. However, something happened that physically separated us. This may have involved a promotion or job change that required a move.

Or perhaps one of our lifestyles or interests changed. Some examples might include:

1. We started a family, and our friend didn't or doesn't plan to.
2. We previously worked together every day, but now we don't.
3. We were roommates in college but haven't regularly connected since graduation.
4. We were childhood friends and only see each other around the holidays when we both go home to visit.

This layer of friendship I call our soul sisters because of the strong emotional connection we share. Many women have a soul sister that they consider to be their very best friend. The cool thing about our sisters in this group is that when we do connect, it's as if we haven't skipped a beat. We are right back where we were when we last met. We often spend time reminiscing over fond memories. The time and space that has separated us has not damaged our connection. Although these relationships are now slow to evolve, they do not lose ground.

These friendships serve us beautifully and add great value. They are the people who know who we used to be. They understand our roots and continue to follow our journey from afar. They can say "Remember when . . ." and have us tapping into our former selves instantly. We are excited for and look forward to our infrequent yet fulfilling reconnects. These occasional opportunities to meet are cherished. If we really needed them, our soul sisters would be there for us, even though we haven't spoken for a while.

This village is an elite group of women. Similar to Tribe, our soul sisters likely amount to a handful or fewer. Again, if not for lack of proximity, these women would be our Tribe. In fact, they probably were a member of our Tribe until we were separated by circumstance. The strong bonds we share make for a lifetime of friendship.

Teri

My friend Teri is one of my soul sisters. We met many years ago in Las Vegas, Nevada, where I had taken a job as a fitness trainer for a Nevada Test Site, supervising the security guard's endurance and strength training. (I also taught an aerobics class. I like to joke with new friends that one of my past jobs was as a dancer in Vegas!) Anyway, after 18 months of 12-hour shifts and a two-hour round trip commute, I decided that job was not for me. At the ripe age of 23, I had no social life in a city that doesn't sleep. I decided to accept a job that would utilize my second degree, business administration, working for Blockbuster Video. (I know . . . that dates me, doesn't it?) Teri was a store manager and trainer for the district's stores. She was assigned to get me up and running and ready to lead a store quickly. Blockbuster was booming with store expansion at the time. Teri was an amazing trainer, and we quickly built a friendship. She is one of those souls who will do almost anything for anyone. A hard worker, Teri is loyal to all of her relationships, business and personal.

As a young twentysomething now with a little more time freedom, it was a great time to live in Las Vegas. Working for Blockbuster Video with Teri was a blast. The atmosphere was lively and energetic, and the video rental business was a significant player in the entertainment industry. We got to talk about MOVIES all day and share our enthusiasm and recommendations with our customers. Teri and I would get to travel to entertainment conventions where we were treated like stars and even rubbed shoulders with a few celebrities at the first annual (of six) Blockbuster Awards. Of course, we were roommates on these adventures, and we had an amazing time together. During our regular workweeks, we would often set similar schedules at our respective stores. After we closed the store at midnight (or 3:00 a.m.), you would likely find us meeting up at Taco Cabana for tacos and a pitcher of frozen margaritas out on their patio. Such fond memories. As I look back, I now know that Teri was my Tribe during that era.

We both continued to grow our careers at Blockbuster. Teri became a district manager in Las Vegas, and I took a job as the new recruiter for the Rocky Mountain

Region. After spending one holiday season working retail in Vegas, my fiancé and I were determined to get back to Colorado. Blockbuster provided the ticket home. The only sad part was leaving Teri and a handful of other friends. At least we still had Blockbuster . . . for a while, anyway.

Teri and I have remained close friends. She was one of my bridesmaids, and I was to be one of hers (if not for being assigned bedrest during my second pregnancy). Teri married a wonderful man and moved to Texas to build their life together with a son and bonus daughter. We both advanced out of Blockbuster before its imminent demise. Now, we stay in touch via social media, texts, and phone calls. Teri's work brings her to Denver on occasion, so we try to get together then. Sometimes she comes out for our GNO Retreat.

A few years back, I received a message from Teri's sister. She shared with me that Teri's husband had suddenly and unexpectedly passed. I tear up as I think back to this moment. I remember becoming overwhelmed with emotion. Although I did not know him well, my empathy for Teri's loss overtook me. I sobbed uncontrollably for some time and then reached for the phone. I feared it would not be a good time to call. She would obviously have so much on her plate and many emotional phone calls. I just had to let her know I was here for her and literally would be there . . . on the next plane . . . if she needed me.

She answered. We cried together. She was obviously in shock but amazingly strong. She had to be. She had to keep it together for her kids and mother-in-law who still lived with her. We decided together that I would come to visit in one month, after the whirlwind of family and local friends swept through. We spent most of our time cooking, eating, and watching chick-flicks on the Hallmark Channel. We just hung out and enjoyed each other's company. We remain soul sisters.

Your Tribe

The first layer, closest to heart-center, is our Tribe. These are the friendships we let into the inner sanctum of our hearts and minds. We trust these ladies with our deepest secrets, and we know they will never betray our trust. They are a powerful force of energy who provide a protected layer of energy, invisible but unmistakably present. *Soul sisters* are far from cliché in a Tribe.

Jane

I want to share about my *Bestie* Jane. As close as we are, she is the newest member of my Tribe. When we met, I was instantly drawn to her. She is a strikingly beautiful woman, the kind that one would naturally feel a little intimidated by. However, she was so open and real that I quickly overcame my own insecurities that she was 'too cool' to be my friend.

One of the reasons I wanted to get to know Jane better was because she openly shared her own insecurities. We were part of a networking group, and each time we met, everyone would have the opportunity to introduce themselves and give an elevator pitch. This *60 seconds of fame* was the only chance we got to create curiosity and connect with listeners in the room. Those who don't love public speaking silently dread this part of the meeting. Back in the day, Jane was in that camp. I remember her sharing her anxiety about being in the spotlight.

For some time, we connected at this monthly meeting, but soon thereafter, our relationship expanded to lunches, happy hours, and travel. I have watched her grow through her public speaking insecurities. Although she still confesses to some butterflies in her stomach, she can speak in front of hundreds appearing cool, calm, and articulate. She has built her business as a realtor from scratch, sharing her fears along the way and even questioning if she would be able to make it in this highly competitive industry. She has been amazing to watch, working so hard for her clients and juggling their many needs and demands. Jane continues to focus on her own personal and professional growth and is truly the best at what she does. Today she has a thriving business, and I am so proud of her.

Jane is one of the most supportive friends I have ever had. No matter what I find myself getting into, she is right there with me, *all in*. No matter how crazy my next adventure or conquest may be, Jane has my back. She cheers me on and represents my best interests when I am not around. She gets me, and that feels so good. Although her career is very demanding of her schedule, she always makes time for me. This kind of loyalty is uncommon, and it's why I cherish my friendship with Jane.

I share this friendship story because it strongly illustrates the components of a Tribal connection. Remember the Tribal formula:

TRIBE = FRIENDSHIP + SPACE + VULNERABILITY

My friendship with Jane did not happen overnight, and we did not immediately begin by sharing our deepest darkest secrets. It took years to establish this trust and confidence in each other. We invested time, gave our relationship the space by connecting regularly, created fond memories, and along the way, shared our hearts.

I think the best Hollywood example of a successful Tribe are the ladies from *Sex and the City*: Carrie, Samantha, Charlotte, and Miranda. The show's creators playfully market the series as all about SEX and the New York City lifestyle. However, make no mistake, what made the series a smash hit was not the character's sexual escapades, but rather, the bonds they created with their sister Tribe. These four ladies shared a connection that wasn't mythical, perplexing, or sexual. Carrie, Samantha, Miranda, and Charlotte shared the greatest love story, grander than any other, with their Tribe. Carrie once suggested that they should be each other's soulmates and just "have fun" with the guys.[34] I believe many real-life sister Tribes would echo this sentiment. Carrie's on-and-off-again boyfriend, Big, suggested that he came in fourth place in Carrie's pecking order as her girlfriends were "the loves of her life".[xxxv] *Sex and the City* taught us how to be real, brave, and honest with our friends. The show is over, but its lessons on friendship live on.

Our Tribe is what girlfriend guru and author Shasta Nelson would call *committed friends*.[35] These are relationships with whom we intimately and consistently share our lives. The term *committed* is purposeful. These are friendships we make room for on a regular basis.

The members of the Tribe are important allies in the pursuit of things like happiness, self-esteem, and well-being. This select group usually amounts to three to five friends. Despite that, as I said before, I hate limits and exclusivity. I always allow room for a +1 because we never know who we are going to meet. Inclusivity and openness are foundational to hit the Friendship

Target. No matter where your number lands, naturally, we hold our tight-knit Tribe closest to our heart-centered core. These are the precious few who make us who we are.

The Core

The center is YOU—the heart of the Friendship Target! You are the core, the choicest, most essential, and most vital part of your sisterhood. This includes your id, ego, super-ego, identity, inner being, psyche, soul, essence, consciousness, and self, to name a few descriptive words. We discussed this in chapter 4, the Leader of your Tribe. You are #1, and a loving relationship with yourself is essential.

At some point in your life, maybe as a young child, you were told that you are NOT the center of the universe. They said, "Stop being selfish, get over yourself, it's not all about YOU!" You probably believed this story. You may have felt a little miffed at first, then embarrassed, and maybe even ashamed of your unwarranted self-interest. From this experience you adapted and began to put others' needs ahead of your own. Well friends, I am here to tell you that proclamation was rubbish, as is the habit of placing you and your needs last.

We share the universe with at least one hundred billion galaxies. We share this earth with almost eight billion other human beings. We are all perfect and equal as created by God, but make no mistake, you *are* the center of your own universe, as am I. This is true not only psychologically but scientifically. Psychologically, we each have our own perspective. We may interpret what is going on around us very differently based on our life experience. There is no other way for us to be, and it is not a selfish standpoint. Our point of view is just that—our point of view. Scientifically, there must be a *center* when a volume of space is measured. Because you reside in the punctual center of your experience, you in fact are the center of your own universe.

So, while it is true that everything in other's lives is not about you, everything in *your* life most certainly is. We should all lean into this reality. By doing so, we can make choices more intentionally that line up with our goals and create the highest version of our self and life experience. You are worthy of love and all good things.

What tendencies have become habits in your life that don't honor you? What areas of your life do you put yourself last and why? If you regularly practice self-sacrifice, it is likely not benefiting anyone as much as it is harming your dignity. Identify these habits and without guilt, begin to choose differently. Abandon patterns of selflessness that don't serve you.

To re-cap, before all others you must know yourself, honor her and care for her without shame or excuse. That is why we spent some time journaling answers about your goals, dreams and perspective. I hope you are reviewing your work, honoring the time you invested in the process, and are considering your answers daily. You need to *get to know* you. You need to love you. You are the substance, sum, essence, meat, gist, marrow, nitty-gritty, and heart and soul of your community. Of course, the core includes only one member. You ARE the center of your own universe and that is as it should be! The world most certainly DOES revolve around you, and don't you forget it!

CHAPTER 7:

Sequential or Serendipity?

LYN HICKS, A WELL-BEING EDUCATOR and author of *The Lotus Project: The Art of Being a Woman* visited with me on the topic of women's well-being and relationships. She is full of wisdom and has an eastern spin on women's wholeness. Lyn conveyed the power of numbers and the triangular sequence as they relate to individuals, friendships, and community.[36]

One

The vibrational essence of the number one is associated with many meaningful attributes including autonomy, optimism, ambition, leadership, birth, and new beginnings. The number one represents a creative and powerful individual whose focus and energy can bring new things into manifestation. The number one is also generally treated as a symbol of unity, God, and the universe.

It is my belief that we are all directly connected to our higher power: God, source energy, the Universe, whatever designation feels right to you. Therefore, we as individuals are also a symbol of the number 1. With this concept in mind, we should welcome and nurture our attributes of independence, positivity, ambition, and leadership. It is our right and responsibility to own our power of one and use our God-given gifts, aspirations, and desires to become whole. In doing so, we can feel complete, have more to give, and live our best life.

If this information sounds familiar, it is true. Nurturing your needs, pursuing your dreams, and following your intuition is crucial—essential not only to your own well-being but to everyone you care about, including your Tribe.

The number one is known not only as an emblem of new beginnings, but also as a sign of motivation, self-leadership, and intuition. If you decide to start a new adventure in your life, you should listen to your inner voice because this is direct communication from source energy.

Caution is due here as to not actively listen to your ego. That is the voice in your head that is critical. The ego is the mind's identity of our own fabrication, an identity that is false. We are more than just the mind and the ego. If we take all the beliefs of who we are: our personality, talents, and abilities, we find the structure of our ego. These aspects of our personality will be characteristics of our being, but the mental image we create of our "self" is artificial. Our ego is an active and dynamic part of our persona, creating sometimes intense emotional drama and self-doubt in our lives.

This is the little voice in our heads that says:

"I'm not good at prioritizing."

"My freckles make me ugly."

"Nobody likes me."

"I don't belong here."

"I am such an idiot."

"I should quit."

Our egos even emit thoughts of being superior in some way:

"I am smarter."

"I am better than her."

The ego hides behind the "I" and "me" in those declaratory thoughts and assertions about our identity. When we agree with even the slightest conviction that these thoughts define us, we are building or reinforcing our egos. If we discover that our egos are showing up often, it's like *our trees* are overgrown in the landscape of our lives. We don't just lift the tree out and throw it away. Instead, we prune it by cutting off manageable pieces to increase our fruitfulness and growth. For example, re-create our own self-criticism statement and instead say: "My freckles make me unique and interesting." The same approach is effective with letting go of the false beliefs that make up the ego. We begin by detaching from individual thoughts that reinforce it, then let go of beliefs, separating ourselves from the false identity of our egos.

On the other hand, our intuition is a gut instinct. It is our immediate understanding of something. There's no need to think it over or get another opinion; we just know. Our purest intuitions are always right. They can show up as a strong feeling to move forward or to halt. Trust your intuition. It is your energy of the number one speaking to you. The number one is powerful, and it is not surprising that it is considered to be one of the most important spiritual, biblical, and prophetic numbers.

Three

The number three represents many wonderful ideas and beliefs. The Holy Trinity is commonly expressed as the statement that one God exists in three equally divine *Persons*: the Father, the Son, and the Holy Spirit. Similarly, a holistic medicine approach—mind, body, spirit—pertains to an individual's mental, physical, and emotional/spiritual health. Three is also the third idea made of the two creating together—like a child is the greater thing that could only become when two individuals come together.

The number three is a primary source of originality and individuation. It is all about abundance and happy communications. This number brings optimism, luck, and an abundance of energy. The number three is perhaps the most prominent number in mythology and folklore. A very packed symbol, the number three also represents the birth-life-death cycle and many other combinations of three, which exemplify an important life journey necessary to complete the soul's objective during this lifetime.

In friendship, the number three is the creation of Tribe. Two individuals can be best friends, but when a third best friend enters the triad, we have a Tribe. An extra person makes for a much more dynamic and complex friendship, albeit a profound and wonderful one. It is the beginning of our support network that will be there to share life's celebrations and difficulties. We should not rely on a single BFF to be our everything. That is a big responsibility. Establishing our Tribe and selectively adding members will strengthen our support systems; each person brings their varying degrees of knowledge, skills, and abilities. Adding just one friendship and creating a Tribe can exponentially enhance our lives. Be aware, however, that the addition of a third BFF can present its own challenges. Practicing open communication and inclusivity is key to its success.

Six

Is it serendipity or mathematical coincidence that six is both the sum $(1 + 2 + 3)$ and the product $(1 \times 2 \times 3)$ of the first three numbers? The number six is, therefore, considered *perfect*. In mathematics, a perfect number is one that equals the sum of its divisors (excluding itself), and six is the first perfect number because its divisors are one, two, and three. The six days of Creation in Genesis, with God resting on the seventh day, illustrate the perfection of six. On day one, light is created;

on days two and three, heaven and earth appear; finally, on days four, five, and six, all living creatures are created. Thus, the structure of the Creation parallels the sum: $1 + 2 + 3 = 6$.[37]

Life Coach and Writer, Fiona Stubbings, contributed an article for *The Thrive Global Community* and believes that in our womanhood, our connection with other women is one of the most beautiful things and benefits our mental health.[38] I concur and suggest that in friendship, although there can be more or less, the number six represents a complete Tribe. It has been said that we become like the five or six people we surround ourselves with most of the time. In that case, don't you think we all need to make sure we have quality people around us who inspire, uplift, and make us better people just by being around them? Fiona shared about her #WarriorWomen Tribe and believes there are six friends every woman needs:[39]

1. ***The Tribal Chief***—This is the woman who is wiser, more experienced at life and always has great advice when it comes to making big decisions. She is usually older but still fun and will guide you lovingly through difficult times.

2. ***The Trail Blazer***—This friend is connected. She knows people and she helps you to get things done. She can link you up with everything from the best reiki master to the latest technology. People love her for her positivity and success.

3. ***The Fan Girl***—This is the friend who is your biggest fan. She likes all your social media posts; she cheers

you on in every new endeavor. She believes in you, thinks you're awesome and sings your praises at every opportunity.

4. *The Empath*—This friend has totally got your back. You can cry on her shoulder, and she will always listen and comfort without judgment or offering unsolicited advice. She is pure love and empathy.

5. *The Truth Doctor*—This is the friend you go to for absolute, no-holds-barred, straight down the line truth about anything. It's the brutal honesty you need when you are all caught up in the emotions. She won't sugar coat, but you know she loves you, and she is invaluable to your life.

6. *The Fun Fitness Friend*—This friend is the one you exercise with. She's essential to your physical and mental health—she will keep you from going to the wine shop on the way home from a stressful day, and she will get you out there running, hiking, paddle boarding, or whatever it is you love to do together to let off steam and have a laugh. You can't live without a fun fitness friend. [40]

Fiona's perspective is spot on; these are great characteristics of women with whom to build your Tribe. My Tribe reflects a blend of these characteristics and more. You can see how a Tribal support system like this could lift you up to reach your higher purpose, and on occasion, catch you when you fall.

Ten

Britannica says the *most* perfect number is considered to be 10, because 10 = 1 + 2 + 3 + 4.[41] This number symbolized unity arising from multiplicity. Moreover, it is related to space. A single point corresponds to one, a line to two (because a line has two extremities), a triangle to three, and space to four. Thus, 10 also symbolizes all possible spaces.[40]

In friendship, the number 10 is considered perfect because it is the sum of the Individual + Tribe + Complete Tribe: 1 + 3 + 6 = 10. Remember that 10+ represents our Kindred Clan, which includes every friendship our Tribe brings to the community. This organic multiplicity of our friendships weaves an interconnected network of support and contacts.

Numerology experts believe that there is a divine or mystical relationship between a number and one or more coinciding events. Numerologists place faith in numerical patterns and draw pseudo-scientific inferences from them. St. Augustine of Hippo (AD 354–430) explained that numbers are a universal language that confirm the truth.[42]

The numbers that make up your Tribe will vary. You may have three, six, eight, or even more. There are no steadfast rules, and the numbers may change over time. Let's consider the "significant" Tribe numbers as only a sequential guideline to our Tribe's serendipity:

SIGNIFICANT TRIBE NUMBERS

1 = YOU—THE INDIVIDUAL
3 = THE BEGINNING OF TRIBE
6 = THE COMPLETION OF TRIBE

10X = THE EXPONENTIAL COMMUNITY OF TRIBE

There are a plethora of books on the topic of numerology as it relates to an individual's life path, love, and other relationships. No matter where your beliefs sit in regards to these data points and numerology, perhaps you find it interesting as well. Not dismissing numerology all together, I believe my friend Michelle would suggest serendipity and divine inspiration guide us to our Tribe.

Michelle

I call Michelle my Soul Seraph because she has an angelic quality about her. We all have a direct connection with our source, however, I feel as if Michelle is able to tune to that energy more readily and share the message of light, ardor, and purity with those blessed to be around her. She adds tranquility, serenity, and peace everywhere she goes. I think of my friendship with Michelle as a fluid conversation, so I asked Michelle to participate in our friendship story.

Brenda

When I met Michelle, she was the pharmacist at our local grocery store. My children were young, and they brought home all kinds of maladies. I think they caught about every ailment you can think of, from the sniffles, coughs, and fevers to broken ankles, warts, and even the dreaded lice. Times thrice. Eww. That one was the worst.

Michelle appeared as this bright light on these dismal occasions when the doctor prescribed his remedy for what felt like the *condition of the month club*. She was always there with a genuine warm greeting and really connected with her customers. She was present, in the moment, and focused on helping us heal.

After some time, I felt a strong urge to get to know Michelle outside of our customer-pharmacist relationship. She always bubbled with great energy. I could tell she was special, and I wanted to be her friend. You could say that her vibe attracted me to her Tribe. I don't exactly remember how it started, but I must have asked for her phone number.

As I recall, the years that we have been friends, are divided into two time periods. The first probably lasted three to five years, and neither of us were at points in our lives that encouraged going too deep. She had a demanding career and was still raising her family. I had two arduous businesses. Following in my mother's footsteps,

I endeavored to be Supermom, working full-time and trying not to miss anything in my kids' lives.

For a few years, I completely lost touch with Michelle. I called and left messages here and there but I did not hear back. We had never expected too much from each other up to this point, but her non-responsiveness was unusual. I was bummed that it seemed that we may have grown apart and I really didn't know why.

Michelle

It's almost impossible to explain why there was a period of absence of close relationship between Brenda and me. Certainly, there was no reason. There was no loss of attraction or kinship. Life happened, and that is all. Children grow like wild strong weeds through concrete, careers crescendo and fall, and my marriage dissolved before my unwilling eyes and heart. Reaching out to friends to advertise my pain never crossed my mind.

One sunshiny day, while taking a walk around the neighborhood lake, an oncoming jogging lady approached and passed by me from the opposite direction. I recognized her with my soul. And just then, she stopped. She halted mid-stride and came back. Brenda came back. My Spirit Bird came back to get me.

Brenda

The next week, we scheduled lunch at a cute new wood-fired pizza place in town. We caught up over a few hours with a gourmet pizza and a couple of beers. We found ourselves going deep fast. She shared some very personal news about significant parts of her life. In learning this, it all made sense. The years of no contact had been full of life changing obstacles of which Michelle was not yet completely through.

Michelle

Reconnecting and reacquainting was effortless. Our "first date" after the never-broke-up season was the kind where time flew, and nothing but our connection mattered. We covered years in hours and had the "never missed a day" kind of feeling that only soul sisters know. I was just beginning to understand that the Universe was in control . . . of everything . . . since my life was so not.

Brenda

I shared with her some of my personal and private journeys as well, including losing my two brick-and-mortar businesses in the great recession of 2008. I told the story of the little old lady who came into my shop on the last day we were open. I had never seen this woman before, and I remember her perfume smelling like my late grandmother's. She looked at me with sympathy and said to me, "Honey, this is not just your business closing; this is your dream dying." She was right. To this day, I believe this message of love and compassion was from my grandmother Grace. This failure did feel like a death of sorts to both myself and to my husband.

Michelle

Brenda was the safe room to my internal panic room, and we told each other the unbelievable that we could not believe ourselves. Somehow, speaking the unspeakable out loud to one another grounded us both. Spiritual paths, emotional ignorance, fallings from grace, and outright miracles . . . we covered it all. All the unacceptable, unimaginable crap . . . was now "out there," and I never felt so loved, respected, and accepted.

Brenda

I told Michelle about the healing journey my family was on and the nontraditional healers to whom we had recently been introduced. I was looking at the way the world works and my place in it in a whole new way. The good and the bad, eastern and western healing, the law of attraction and allowing versus resisting. At this very moment, Michelle was in complete alignment with me on this journey. This moment changed our friendship forever.

Michelle

We started at Point A and covered straight through to Z in one pizza and two beers' time. Nothing was missed or wasted on one another. There was no judgment and not a second lost, despite the years we'd journeyed independently. Brenda and I had walked so many paths, side by side in heart, only two miles apart.

Brenda

From that point on, Michelle and I kept close tabs on each other. We were both still very busy with all other aspects of our lives, but we made the intentional effort to connect regularly. For years now, Michelle has been my confidante, hiking partner, counselor, soft spot to land and the soul seraph of my Tribe.

Michelle

Our Spirits were back together and better, stronger, and faster than they'd ever been before as "friendlies."

And THAT is when the real Lady and the Tribe began.

From that day forward—whether it's our annual Girls' Weekend in the mountains, a monthly Women Who Wine, a private New Year's Eve party, a healing circle ceremony, or just another walk around the same lake—Brenda and I have been soundly and solidly IN each other's Tribes.

Brenda

Well said Michelle. Thank you my, friend. Namaste.

CHAPTER 8:

A Recipe for Tribe

What does it require to take a relationship Tribal? It is not difficult, but it does require an intentional effort focusing on four key elements. Let's spend some time breaking down the Tribal formula:

TRIBE = FRIENDSHIP + SPACE + VULNERABILITY

TIME—THE CONTINUUM OF EXPERIENCE IN WHICH EVENTS PASS FROM THE FUTURE THROUGH THE PRESENT TO THE PAST.[43]

We all spend time on many useful—and perhaps many more useless—things. Instead of *spending* time, *invest* time in people and projects that create positive proceeds. We invest in something that has value and is important to us. In this way, the time we spend becomes an investment and not an expense. An investment of time in a friendship is the first step in moving it toward Tribe.

Here's the problem. No matter who you are, where you live, or whether you are married, single, parent, professional, retired, man, or woman, we all are limited to a mere 24 hours per day and 168 hours per week. Time is our most precious resource. With our busy lives filled with a multitude of commitments and the myriad of competing priorities, it is understandable why our friendships have taken a back seat. The squeaky wheel gets the grease, right? If it isn't a boss asking us to work overtime, it's our spouse negotiating carpool responsibilities or our daughter's incessant, "Mom . . . mom . . . mom . . . mom . . . " Our faithful but often silent friendships don't demand our attention, and because of that, they take a back seat and often don't even make the trip.

As we age, the time we spend with friendships declines from more than 30% as a teenager, to 8% as a retiree. The lowest numbers are for 40–65 year olds, who average only 4%.[44] Think about this statistic. In a week, 4% of 168 hours is 6.72 hours. Does that seem low or high to you? Considering the loneliness epidemic we are facing, I bet 4% is a big stretch for many people.

When time is limited, we just aren't able to connect with everyone we want to as often as we would like. We need to identify what relationships are most important and who beyond our family is worthy of our most limited resource. If we do not make this conscious decision for ourselves, the decision will be made for us. Think about the time you get caught up in social media just looking around at everyone else's *published* life instead of living your own. For many, this probably adds up to more than 6.72 hours per week. I have been guilty myself. It is addicting! If this is you, don't beat yourself up about it. Make a new choice. A funny meme said, "Never blame anyone for the road you are on. That's your own asphalt."[45] I do hope your road trip is going well. If it's not, make a decision and turn toward what you want. You will get there!

Thinking about our limited time and how it gets eaten up with other people's priorities, minutia, and our own disorganization, it reminds me of our 34th President's decision matrix. President Dwight Eisenhower suggested that the "urgent" things in our life are usually not that important.[46]

Doesn't this ring true when you really think about it? When we are healthy, taking care of ourselves is not URGENT, but oh, so important. Our friends are not demanding of our time, but the moments spent with them are the most fulfilling and meaningful. On the other hand, the incessant *notifications* we get when an email is delivered, or someone *likes* our post are distractions that steal our time away. Eisenhower created a matrix ranking tasks on two key characteristics:

1. The importance of the task to the overall success of the mission

2. The urgency with which the task needs to be carried out

He divided the way we spend our time into four quadrants: important and urgent, important but not urgent, not important but urgent, and not important and not urgent. This broad framework can be applied to a wide range of situations and is popular for many time management gurus.[47] Take a look at the diagram as we will discuss it further.

Eisenhower, who had also served as a General in the United States Army as the Allied Forces Supreme Commander during World War II, created this matrix sometime around his

Presidency in 1953. He was described as the embodiment of productivity and time management, which led him to establishing the above famous matrix. I took some liberties and updated Quadrant 3 with "other people's problems" instead of "activities" and Quadrant 4 to omit "trivia" and "pleasant activities" with "social media" and "distractions."

As you can see, we want to live our lives as much as possible in Quadrant 2: *investing* our time in relationships, planning, and recreation. This includes things like our health, exercise, personal development, and time with family and friendships.

Here are some strategies to reduce or eliminate wasted time.

Quadrant 1—Important and Urgent (DO):
- Like Nike says . . . "Just Do It!"
- Usually this is an emergency
- When the house is on fire, you better grab a bucket of water

Quadrant 2—Important but Not Urgent (DECIDE):
- Schedule it!
- Brainstorming, strategy, dreaming, planning
- Personal and professional development, training, learning
- Quality time with family, investing in friendships, Tribe-time
- Do this well, and you will have less of Quadrant 1 to deal with

Quadrant 3—Not Important, Urgent (DELEGATE):

- Who can do this for you?
- Push back someone else's urgent deadline.
- Avoid the urgency trap! This is usually busy work; avoid it at all cost! If you accept it, you are first on the list for next time.
- Turn off all of those notifications! Emails, texts, and social media bleeps beeps and buzzes interrupt and distract you. Refocusing is a time waster.
- Investing too much time in shallow friendships, reassign this time to your Tribe.

Quadrant 4—Not Important, Not Urgent (DELETE):

- "Just *Don't* Do It!"
- Eliminate it.
- If this is a guilty pleasure (social media), put a plan in place to seriously limit the time you spend. You will never get those scrolling and stalking hours back.

Invest your time in Quadrant 2 by creating a plan that will allow you to maximize your schedule and make time for your Tribe. How much time do you need to set aside? Well, that depends on how long you want it to take to create significant, resonant friendships. A 2018 study published in the *Journal of Social and Personal Relationships* calculated that you must spend about 50 hours with someone before you consider them a casual friend. It takes 90 hours before you become real friends. When you hit 200 hours, you finally hit the close friendship mark.[48] You can spread relationship-building time over days, weeks, months, years, or decades. It's up to you.

One week is 168 hours. Let's assume you spend 8 hours sleeping every night, so back out 56 hours for a waking balance of 112 hours. Budget in a 50-hour workweek for your income producing activities leaving you 62 hours of personal time each week. Our personal lives can be quite hectic. Demanding even! However, if you don't schedule your discretionary time with your own priorities, Quadrant 3 will take over, and other people will! If you are just beginning, it's okay to start small and work your way up. Just be sure to start! Time is the #1 indicator of successful relationships. How important are your friendships right now? How important do you want them to be?

SPACE—AN AREA RESERVED FOR AND BOUND BETWEEN PEOPLE.

Another key indicator of a successful Tribe is proximity, which we will refer to in our equation as space. This is where we give our friendships the room and place to grow. Geography will not only influence who becomes a friend, but with whom we maintain and grow in friendship.

Many believe that the technology revolution has reduced the importance of geographical proximity. They claim that people no longer need to meet each other physically or in person. With the birth of social media, texting, free long-distance phone calls, and video chats, some say that it is possible to think of the world with no territorial barriers. However, research has proven otherwise. In a 2009 study by Goldbert and Levy, with a database of 100,000 Facebook users, found that communication decreases with geographical distance.[49] A similar study determined that spatial vicinity has a great impact on how individuals create their connections on online social platforms. More active social media users also tend to interact more often with people who live nearby.

It appears "the closer, the better" when it comes to creating deep, meaningful relationships. There have been studies in classrooms, businesses, and police academies that all find the same results . . . nothing will prove as influential as the shortest distance between friendships. Think about it. If you have a current BFF, how did you meet her? Did you frequent the same networking event? Were you assigned to sit next to her in class? Did you work in the same department? How did your friendship grow? Was it texting and chatting over social media, or did you share some life experience on a somewhat regular interval together in person? It is likely that you bonded one-on-one over the years with coffee and lunch dates, happy hours, long walks, shopping, and sharing chick-flicks.

Let's face it. Sometimes we just need a hug! Hugs positively impact both our mental and physical health. Not everyone is comfortable with the same level of physical touch, but regardless, there are many reasons we should get and give more hugs on a daily basis:

- Hugs may boost immunity, reducing the chance that you will get sick and mitigate the severity of cold symptoms and less-severe illness signs.
- Hugs may lower stress. Feeling a conflict coming on? Hugging reduces stress not only in the person being comforted but also the person doing the comforting. Hug it out!
- Hugs may boost your heart health by lowering blood pressure levels and heart rate. The stress hormone norepinephrine has been recorded when a hug was added to the mix.
- Hugs may increase your self-esteem. Bonding and socially connecting via hugs can bolster your self-esteem by giving and receiving love.
- Hugging promotes trust. Embracing releases the hormone oxytocin, which elevates stress and promotes relaxation resulting in a substantial increase in trust.
- Hugs can reduce anxiety. Touch can reduce fear and promote connection.
- Hugging can make you happy. Also known as the *cuddle hormone*, oxytocin is associated with happiness.
- Hugging may reduce depression. Emotional attachment and intimacy are the cornerstones of happy, healthy long-term friendships. Serotonin, which is a natural antidepressant, is released with a hug .
- Hugs may help reduce pain. When a mother or nurse gently strokes the arm of a child who is about to receive the shot, she expresses care and love and distracts the

child from the pain. Hugs can work the same way.
- Hugging may be critical to survival. Deprived of physical touch, babies, and sometimes animals, can experience *failure to thrive*, resulting in depression.
- Hugging shows appreciation. Time spent touching or hugging can have quantifiable neuro-biological benefits.
- Hugs help you communicate. Hugging is a powerful expression of love and connections.

Experts suggest that we need a minimum of four hugs a day just to survive, eight for maintenance, and twelve for growth.[50] Even prior to the introduction of social distancing, we in western civilization were already touch deprived, living alone or just too busy for social connection and touching. For optimal health, get as many hugs in each day as you can. There is just no substitute for physical touch, whether it be a quick squeeze or a long embrace.

The power of touch can quickly connect us in a deep and meaningful way. Our bodies are our most powerful organ and are our best tool for achieving genuine intimacy. All of the benefits of hugging would not be possible if not for proximity. People who share a physical space—and hugs—are more likely to develop meaningful friendships.

Enthusiasm—A lively interest.

We are all sensitive to energy and are drawn to individuals who put out positive vibes in our direction. That is why we all adore our pets who greet us with exuberance when we return from another room. A warm jump for joy from a child when she recognizes you is so natural to her and so affirming to us. It feels good to be seen, appreciated, and adored.

When it comes to the energy that one puts out, I am reminded of the BNI (Business Networking International) organization's philosophy *Givers Gain®*. It is based on the old adage "what comes around goes around" and implies that by giving business, we will receive business in return. The same goes for the energy we put out into the world. How are you showing up? Who are you attracting? There are three types of *energies* we may encounter. Author Adam Grant identifies them as the givers, the takers, and the matchers.[51]

First, let's discuss an energy you are blessed to encounter. They are the givers. These contributors are focused on others. Their support and sacrifice comes with no strings attached. These folks have wide networks and build the deepest bonds in their relationships. Their fan base is extensive, and everyone cheers them on, offering encouragement and assistance if needed. Reciprocity for the giver is organic, a natural result of being a contributor and making a difference. It goes without saying, the rewards of life come their way because they are attracting them resistance free. Givers are usually the most successful and happiest. They live life with enthusiasm and share it with everyone that they encounter.

Next let's chat about the takers. They try to acquire as much as possible from their interactions while giving as little as they can in return. Takers struggle to feel genuine happiness for another person. Instead, they prefer to pull energy to feed their emotional demands. These folks are often needy and drain others of their energy while sharing complaints and problems. They are not necessarily conscious that they are sponging up our energy, and they may be in an emotionally unstable state through no fault of their own. Regardless, energy theft can harm both the perpetrator and the victim. These are the receivers or leeches, and you can never do enough to help or fix them. Also known as energy vampires, takers can show up in many forms, described well by Alfred James on his website pocketmindfulness.com:52

1. **Dominator vampires** have a number of insecurities around being hurt, wronged, or weakened by others, so they try to conceal the emotional trauma by dominating and taking control of others.

2. **Judgmental vampires** feed their ego by highlighting and making fun of your insecurities until you feel pathetic and small.

3. **Melodramatic vampires** have the need to create drama, mainly because they need to feed the void they feel inside. They love a crisis and being involved in problematic situations. They thrive on being victimized and therefore are in need of attention and love. Your energy will be drained when you get sucked into the drama they create.

4. **Narcissistic vampires** lack empathy for others and have a need for admiration. They don't have a genuine

interest in others. They are manipulative. They charm you, leaving you powerless to fend off their influence to put them first at all costs and massage their ego.

5. **Victim vampires** target you through guilt. Usually, this type of person has remarkably low self-esteem. They believe that their suffering is mainly due to others, so instead of taking responsibility for their lot in life, they blame and emotionally pressure others.

6. **Innocent vampires** aren't aware that they're stealing the energy of those around them. Good examples are your overly dependent friends who rely on you a bit too much. While it's great that you show compassion to these people, it's important to motivate them to be self-reliant.

The key to dealing with a taker or an energy vampire is to recognize them and not invite them. Ultimately, you have control of your time and what you will and won't give to other people. If you must interact, set limits and don't let them suck the life out of you!

The third energy you might encounter are the matchers. These individuals are the scorekeepers and give when it is to their advantage to do so. They like to maintain an equal balance of giving and taking. Let's be fair—this is reciprocity at its best, with mutual action and reaction. The matchers play an important role in our society and realistically make up the majority of the population. They make sure what comes around goes around. This is good for the givers. Matchers will reward givers for their generous behavior and seek revenge when they or others are being mistreated. The taker's behavior will not go unrecognized for long by the matchers. See ya!

Now having reviewed the three energy types, I ask you again, how are you showing up for your friendships? Ideally in most of our interactions, we are both giving and getting. We are showing up with enthusiasm, to connect, share, laugh, and even vent sometimes. Oxytocin is released with a big hug, and almost immediately we feel more relaxed and appreciated. We listen, validate, and encourage each other, departing happier than before we got together.

Although it is likely we are often matchers (most people are), when it comes to your closest friendships, approach them with a giver's mindset. Show your BFF's your excitement to see them and eagerness to spend time together. Let's face it, when we give to our friendships, we are really benefiting ourselves in a meaningful way. We are each other's *soft spot to land,* and most of the time, our communication should overflow with eagerness, enjoyment, and approval. This habit of optimism with our besties builds on itself so that when disagreements or conflict occur (which realistically is not an *if* but a *when*), you have the foundation of positivity to anchor your friendship. Next time you get to see your Tribe or BFF, try greeting them with the excitement of a toddler or a puppy dog and see how that impacts the evening. Beyond our basic physiological and safety needs, what we long for is to be seen, heard, loved, and to belong. We should be a reflection for each other, acknowledging our significance and contribution to the Tribe.

VULNERABILITY—THE STATE OF BEING VULNERABLE, TRANSPARENT OR EXPOSED.[53]

This can be a scary one, ladies, and I believe it may be the reason more women do not have close lifelong friendships. In a world where everyone is pretending to have it all together, exposing our problems, fears, and inadequacies is frightening. There are exceptions, of course, but most people do not advertise their troubles and shortcomings. Beyond that, the secrets, shame, and transgressions that sometimes make up our private "real" life . . . well that information is often reserved and shared only on a need-to-know basis.

We have been socialized to share the good stuff. Many of us were raised to not cause or speak of trouble. Mind your own business and keep it positive. When asked, "How are you?" the response is usually "Good," "Great," or "Busy!" Certainly, don't get real and overshare. We were taught that no one wants to hear confessions of our deepest struggles and conflicts.

In addition to enculturation, there are lots of reasons we are afraid to go deep. Fear of rejection is one. What if the real me is just not good enough? What if my truth is just too offensive? Will I be judged? Will I still fit in? Can I trust her with my biggest secrets? Will she betray my confidence? What would happen if *everyone* knew my secret? Would they laugh and talk about me behind my back? What will people think? Could I lose everything? Our mind becomes a runaway freight train with all the "what ifs" and worst-case scenarios.

Another reason is shame. Our internal dialogue tells us,

"I'm bad. There's something wrong with me. I'm broken. I'm unworthy. I'm not enough." Author and shame expert Brené Brown describes shame as sensing and believing that we are not enough. This belief makes us feel that we would be rejected if the other person really *knew* us. She also says that vulnerability is emotional exposure, an uncertain risk.[54] This vulnerability thing doesn't sound fun at all! Why must we go there?

Our fears prevent us from being our authentic self and totally engaging in the friendship. Being vulnerable helps us ask for what we want without shutting down or distancing from friendships. It allows us to build trust in others and to become fully engaged in an intimate relationship. Being vulnerable allows us to open our heart to give and receive love fully and be seen.

Terry Gaspard's blog on *Your Tango* lists the top reasons why vulnerability in a relationship can lead to intimacy.[55] Vulnerability can:

1. Increase our sense of worthiness and authenticity
2. Help us feel close and connected to our friendships
3. Help us communicate what we want
4. Allow us to build trust in others and gain intimacy
5. Allows us to give and receive love fully.

So how do we make the shift? We begin by caring and loving ourselves first. (An excellent start is the exercise we completed in chapter 5 of this book entitled The Leader of Your Tribe). So much of this work starts with learning about yourself and understanding what makes YOU tick. Love yourself enough to continue reviewing your answers on a daily basis. You are the star of your own story. Honor your preferences, your passions, and do things that make you happy. Forgive yourself for mistakes made in the past and be proud of the life lessons that brought you to where you are now. When you are in a good authentic place with YOU, only then can you build genuine devoted friendships.

If you are new to opening up, perhaps a little practice would help. If you want to get started, Amanda Fuel suggests choosing someone you like (doesn't even have to be someone you adore or highly respect; "just likeable" is a great place to start). Then, share something that you've not shared before—something true that you'd like to someday share with a close girlfriend. And see how it feels to be known at that deeper level by someone else.[56]

From there, you can experiment with people you like even more. Understand that your results may vary, and some will not respond in the warm accepting way you hope for. That's okay. Those are not your peeps! However, there will be people who do respond with genuine care and attention. Maybe they will then feel safe enough to share something vulnerable and meaningful with you too. These are your peeps. They get you. And it can be so wonderful to have these genuine connections.

Take it slow and start small. It is not advised to jump into the vulnerability deep end too quickly. Oversharing when a relationship is new or not ready will not get you to the finish line faster. Have you ever been in a situation when someone shared something private, and you didn't have the history or context to understand? Awkward! It's likely you thought, "Wow, what am I supposed to do with this info?" and quickly found an exit strategy. Going deep too soon may result in the opposite of what we are going for. It can instead create distance because the new friend is uncomfortable. They may discretely slip away never to be seen again. Vulnerability is the last element of the equation for a reason. Once you have established a friendship foundation by spending time together on a somewhat consistent basis and you have built up your connection with enthusiasm, then you gradually begin sharing on a deeper level.

From there vulnerability can be added to your friendships a little at a time. As your friendship evolves by spending time together, gradually communicate some of your realities and truths. It may feel awkward at first to expose your personal issues, problems, and fears. Sharing a secret is telling someone, "Here's a little piece of me; sharing it means I like you." Once you have shared and it is received with kindness, understanding, and validation, you will be grateful for the relief of unloading that secret. It feels incredible to be seen, heard, and accepted in that way.

In her book *Frientimacy*, Shasta Nelson suggests that we retrain our brain to assume acceptance from our closest friends.[57] Keep an open heart, and when in doubt, assume the best intentions. Our friends know, like, and trust us. Real love and connection require some risk-taking. Wrongs of the past can be mended with meaningful connection.

The recipe for a Tribe has only four ingredients. Just like baking a cake, it will not rise to the occasion if an ingredient is missing or inadequate. Use high quality ingredients! The care in which you combine your ingredients makes a difference. Bon Appetit!

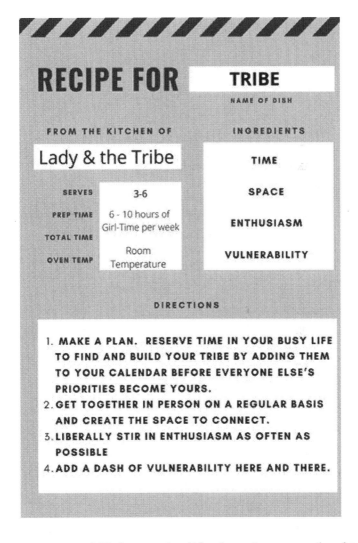

RECIPE FOR — TRIBE
NAME OF DISH

FROM THE KITCHEN OF — INGREDIENTS

Lady & the Tribe — TIME

SERVES — 3-6 — SPACE

PREP TIME — 6 - 10 hours of Girl-Time per week — ENTHUSIASM

TOTAL TIME

OVEN TEMP — Room Temperature — VULNERABILITY

DIRECTIONS

1. MAKE A PLAN. RESERVE TIME IN YOUR BUSY LIFE TO FIND AND BUILD YOUR TRIBE BY ADDING THEM TO YOUR CALENDAR BEFORE EVERYONE ELSE'S PRIORITIES BECOME YOURS.
2. GET TOGETHER IN PERSON ON A REGULAR BASIS AND CREATE THE SPACE TO CONNECT.
3. LIBERALLY STIR IN ENTHUSIASM AS OFTEN AS POSSIBLE
4. ADD A DASH OF VULNERABILITY HERE AND THERE.

A nurtured Tribe can be life changing to each of its members. Friendships matter. Our chores and responsibilities will always be there. Career success will fade in later years. Money will come and go, but friendships only make us richer.

Lifelong Friends

They met at a local park in Texas the summer before third grade. Melinda, once again the "new kid" in town, was scoping out the neighborhood when she came across this beautiful, long-legged girl. Tall, blonde Angela immediately invited Melinda, "Let's ride bikes together!" Melinda was grateful to have been welcomed by this girl who was so kind and offered her big-hearted southern hospitality. "I was a little traumatized from moving from Seattle to Wisconsin and now Texas," Melinda shares. "I remember feeling that once I met Ange, I knew Texas was going to be okay."

From that moment on, the girls were inseparable and grew up together. Even in high school when their interests diverged, and they didn't run with the same pack, Angela and Melinda connected a few times every week. Each knew the other was always there for her. Angela describes, "Riding bikes, going to the pool, having sleepovers, laughing, listening to music, and enjoying Mel's mom's baking were some of my earliest fond memories of 'us.'"

"With Ange, I could be totally myself," Melinda confesses. Angela helped Melinda be less of a perfectionist, and she admits, even get a little goofy. "I needed that because it was hard to move around as a kid and repeatedly start over." Angela helped Melinda "fit in" quickly and feel excepted at school. "It just didn't matter what we were doing, whether it was eating Mr. Daddy's pizza or slathering up with baby oil and basking in the Texas sun. We always had fun together."

Melinda has accepted Angela's typecast, "the extrovert" in the friendship. "I'm the drag you to go do stuff girl," says Melinda. "Although Angela loves to go out and have fun, she has a shy streak."

"I always love glomming on to Mel's fun-bubble," Angela explains. "Mel was always going somewhere and knew all the people. She pulled me out of my comfort zone, more than I would have on my own."

Although their friendship was rock solid, one summer Melinda and Angela experienced some heartache at the same time in their respective homes. Inconceivably, they found themselves in the same predicament. Their parents got divorced the same summer. "It wasn't a shock to me because there was a lot of turmoil happening at my house," Angela shares. "However, it shocked the hell out of me about Mel's parents because I felt like her home was what family was supposed to be like: mama's in the kitchen; dad's funny and he is around. Watching what I perceived as a happy family fall apart almost rocked me to my core, even more than my own parents' divorce."

Melinda and Angela bonded deeply over that summer. They were like sisters, going through the turmoil together. After high school, Angela and Melinda lived together for a bit. Angela married young, at twenty-one. It was a complete disaster and only lasted three years. She moved in with Melinda when she filed for divorce. Angela was sad, depressed, and felt defeated. "Mel had this tiny little apartment, so small, but she graciously shared everything and made me feel at home." A few months later, they moved to a nice apartment that they shared. Angela continues, "It was a blast and vital to my healing process . . . being with Mel and her fun-bubble and not all by myself. She lifted me up during that time when I was broken."

A few years ago, Melinda faced some medical challenges and was told by a brilliant doctor "what's wrong with you is going to require help that is beyond me." Finding solutions required travel out of state to a specialist who sees patients from all around the world. Melinda recalls Angela's encouragement, "Girl, don't worry. I got you. I am going to that appointment with you. It's going to be just fine." On the outside other people probably thought, "Melinda's fine, she is handling herself... but I was pretty terrified," Melinda admits.

Melinda turns to Angela, "You supported me exquisitely, even when it wasn't fun stuff. You flew up here and took care of me after surgery. You went to un-fun, scary doctor appointments with me. You took me into your home. Through it all, you made it all so much better because your beautiful face was there, and I knew that you had me. Words cannot describe those moments. They were beyond meaningful to me. You have made my life so much better. I can't imagine having gone through all of that without you Ange. You made me so much more confident. You really made me believe that everything was going to be okay in a moment when at the core of me, the 'silver lining girl' that I am, I really felt unsure about what my future held. I love you."

"Now Mel . . . I hear it in your voice. Don't you make me cry! I love you too."

Throughout the interview, they referred to each other as "my girl." Today Angela and Melinda face the challenge of being separated by more than 700 miles. Melinda says it can be hard sometimes, "Thank god she married someone that I love," confesses Melinda.

"She married my older brother's best friend, so I always say, 'My brother from another mother married my sister by choice.'"

Although we determined that they first met in third grade, Melinda concludes, "The truth is I can't remember life without my girl, Ange."

CHAPTER 9:

The Impact of Social Media

THE WORLD WIDE Web has unlimited storage and, like the universe, has no edge or boundaries. In our hyperconnected world today, have you ever wondered why we seem more divided than ever? The answer lies in two short words: social media. In its infancy, social media was to be an escape from the real world. Now the real world has become an escape from social media.

I'm trying to think back to my life before social media. I remember my pre-social media life (PSM) and after-social media life (ASM), but I don't remember much about how I got started. It seems almost like it *happened to me* overnight. In 1997, Six Degrees was the first recognizable social media site. It allowed users to make *friends* with other users and upload a profile.[58] I remember the game Six Degrees of Kevin Bacon in the mid-90s, but I have never heard of this social media site. I do remember MySpace, which was created in 2003. I never explored this new universe at the time for a few reasons. First, I was a new mom, overwhelmed . . . enough said. Second, most of the news I heard about MySpace was negative: pedophiles, stalking, bullying, identity theft and slander summed it up. Not for me, no thank you!

Facebook started in February of 2004 on the campus of Harvard University and grew over the next few years to other global colleges and universities. It wasn't until September of 2006 that Facebook opened up for the general public. It seems that things really took off for this social media giant in 2008 when they released Facebook Chat and then a Facebook Wall. In December of 2009 Facebook hit a major milestone by becoming the most popular social platform in the world with 350 million registered users.[59]

I am searching my own Facebook account right now to see when I got started. One of the first posts I see is November 19, 2008. It was from my sister, Bobbi, and stated, "I need to post a picture, I guess. Can you help?" That makes me chuckle but feels about right. Around this time, I see a post reconnecting me to an old high school friend, another to a college friend, and a comment to my mother-in-law's sister, "Hi Suzanne! This is all new to me too but fun!"

From my perspective, this is one of the best things about social media. Facebook has notably revived many dormant relationships. No matter where you stand on the opinions of social media's impact, it would be hard to deny that many of us have enjoyed reconnecting to these old relationships. It makes me wonder what it would be like to have had social media my whole life. What is it like to start collecting an inventory of friends as soon as you have access to a cell phone or computer? What would it be like to never lose connection completely because everyone is linked for a lifetime in your social media network? I guess the coolness of the reconnection piece will, for the most part, be lost on kids born ASM.

Petra

My very first best friend's name is Petra, and I have never been able to find her on social media. We were born three days apart but met for the first time at the age of five on Danbury Drive when my family moved to Colorado from Kansas. We lived on the same street for only one year but remained close friends for years until her family moved to Oklahoma City. Petra was a very special friend to me, my first non-family companion. We spent every playful moment together dreaming up imaginative games and activities.

I remember during this time there was a TV commercial about long-distance telephone calling. It featured two old ladies on the phone having a grand time catching up. We promised each other over and over that we were going to be like those old ladies one day. When her family moved from Longmont to Loveland (less than 20 miles away), we made a plan to meet in Berthoud to celebrate our birthdays because it was the town right between us. It made perfect sense to us . . . Birth-hood" for our birthdays . . . duh! We also decided that if you ate a kernel of unpopped popcorn, you would eventually have a popcorn bay . . . obviously. I don't have the best memory, but these little silly moments remain intact.

A few years into our friendship, I was diagnosed with a very rare and strange but treatable condition that landed me in the hospital for a week or so. Kids were not allowed in the hospital rooms at the time, but Petra wanted to visit me. I remember she convinced her parents to find my hospital room window. They were successful in locating me, and we both squealed with delight when we saw each other. Petra brought me a big balloon that she attempted to push-squeeze through the narrow slat of the screenless window. I can't remember if the balloon made it through, but I remember the determined look on Petra's face to give me that gift! I am laughing to the point of tears as I remember and write this friendship story.

Petra, wherever you are, thank you for your friendship. I will never forget you. But dang it! Why can't I find you on social media, girl? To my readers, if you know a Petra, please ask her if she ever lived in Longmont, Colorado, and if so, please have her look me up! It's not too late for us to enjoy catching up over that long phone call we promised!

Reconnecting with old friends, classmates, and coworkers definitely scores on the plus side of the social media debate. However, what is the verdict on how it is impacting our other relationships? There are many debates going on and from what I have discovered, it continues to be very much a matter of opinion. Has the overuse of the word *friend* devalued the relationships it describes?

Many of us can agree that using cell phones hurts the quality of our time when we are with others: our spouse, children, and girlfriends. No matter who we are with, we need to be mindful of the effect on others when we are absorbed in our phones and social media. We need eye contact to maintain a strong, quality relationship. Eye contact triggers the social networks in our brains that help us create deep connections.

I must admit, I have been guilty of having my nose in my iPhone while with others, especially when I am with my husband. What a terrible message to send. Basically, it's like saying, "Social media has my attention right now even though our time together is limited, and you are here with me now." Boo! I can do better. We must do better!

Over their lifetime, our children are going to be the best subjects to really discover what technology is doing to our relationships. One UCLA study showed that children's social skills may be declining as they spend more time on devices.[60] Another review of 72 social research topics by the University of Michigan found that empathy among college students has decreased 40% over the past 30 years, with the most imposing changes occurring in the past decade when cell phones became pervasive.[61]

For those of us born before 2000, we can remember what our lives were like PSM, pre-cell phones, and pre-text messaging. As kids we spent our free time with friends in the neighborhood dreaming up games and using our imaginations to create mini adventures. We would explore, capture, and investigate bugs and play in the mud. We would play with dolls, have tea parties, and color with crayons. When we were home with family, we were present because there was nowhere else to be. Our lives seemed much more segmented. Wherever you were, your attention and focus would be there too. We would learn things from life experience, of course, but much of our learning came from seeking information.

Today, thanks to technology, information is literally and constantly coming *at* us. The speed of technological advancement is accelerating. We now create as much information every two days as we did in an entire year prior to 2003.[62]

With this perpetual information overload, it is no wonder that we are overwhelmed and sometimes feel as if we are spinning out of control. Social media is only partially to blame for our overconsumption of information. However, marketers have figured out that we spend much of our time there. The frontal assault of marketing warfare has become a blood sport competition for our attention. We are under endless attack, and the marketers are on the winning team.

Here's the rub: we love it. WE have become addicted to the onslaught of information and distraction. Some even rival our cravings and fixation to our mobile devices to that of sex, drugs, and alcohol.

Here are some interesting statistics on digital distraction:[63]

- Over 50% of smartphone owners never switch off their phone.
- 69% of smartphone users check their device within the first five minutes of waking up in the morning.
- 75% of smartphone users admit that they have texted while driving at least one time.
- 44% of adults will check work-related emails while they're on vacation.
- The average smartphone user checks their phone 63 times a day.
- 67% of people check their phone for messages, alerts, or calls—even when they don't notice their phone ringing or vibrating.

Do you resemble any of these statistics? Constant interruptions can have the same effect as the loss of a night's sleep.

I used to think I was a good multitasker. In fact, I was so proud of this gift that I listed it on my resume. Now we have learned that multitasking is a myth. We cannot do or think two things at the same time, so multitasking is impossible. What we are actually doing is switching rapidly between different activities. Each time we switch focus, we lose momentum, and this constant back-and-forth is not good for our clarity, our stress levels, or our relationships. For me, years of trying to multitask have resulted in my having the attention of a squirrel. If I do not intentionally focus, I am easily distracted.

The myth of multitasking is why we believe we can be in the same room with a friend and check our phones at the same time. But . . . we can't. Technology and social media can be an addiction and detract from what is really important. Dare we say that technology and social media have also made us a little bit lazier and more distracted when it comes to our friendships?

As with any addiction, the first step to recovery is recognizing that you have a problem. "Hello, my name is Brenda, and I am a social-tech-oholic." When I figured out that these bad habits were affecting my relationships and productivity, the first thing I did was turn off all those pesky notifications. Every time I would get an email or receive a "Like" or comment on a Facebook post, I used to get a beep, ding, harp, or horn noise that would distract me. Email can wait until the time I have carved out in my schedule. Let's face it: I don't need to know instantly that Sally just liked the good morning puppy dog meme I posted earlier.

What about all the social media friends that you have? If you are like me, the number far exceeds what scientists have determined as our limit of 150. Are all of the additional connections and conversations really distractions from our real life, *in-person* friendships? Well, I think we all can agree that using cell phones and checking social media while we are with our friends can hurt the quality of our relationship. Are we so bewitched by our technology that we not only change what and how we do things, but we change who we are? In her *Ted Talk*, Sherrie Turkle noted that over the last 30 years, she has studied how technologies are transforming our relationships. She finds that technology is making us forget what is important in life—namely intimate conversations and time spent together. The more time we spend texting, emailing, or on social media, the less time we have to speak to our friends in person.[40] Our instant gratification culture has distorted our expectations of the time it takes for intimate friendships to evolve. We are instantly connected by social media, however, lasting relationships take time to create. The most humanizing thing we do is interact face-to-face.[64]

The Problems with Social Media

Social media can promote a false sense of connection. Going back to the sheer numbers, having a thousand friends on Facebook does not indicate the number of close friends in our lives. We may have an abundance of deep acquaintances, but true friendship is built on time spent in conversation and sharing life experiences together. It is commonly thought that social media increases our connections, however, several studies show that people who spend more time on social media are actually more lonely, not less.

Another negative aspect of social media is that it can create feelings of inadequacy. It is quite common to find that many people paint a picture that everything is great, when in fact, things could be quite different—or at least very much up and down. We share as if we have this exciting adventurous life filled with fun, friends and travel. Online, we portray the versions of ourselves that we want people to see. We generally do not share the everyday doldrums of our lives. The behind the scenes work and minutiae that makes it all possible doesn't make it to your Instagram feed. By showcasing only one, sometimes very small portion of our life, we promote an incomplete identity. We then compare our lives to the lives of others—which are seemingly much more interesting—and feel inadequate.

One more area that seems to fall on the negative side of the social media scorecard is what is referred to as FOMO, a colloquial acronym meaning *fear of missing out*. Your close friendships are likely to have other friends and circles that they socialize with because each of us is the leader of our own Tribe. Because it is common to broadcast the fun stuff, you may see them hanging out without you on occasion. In fact, you may see a photo of your two BFFs having lunch . . . without you! Even if you are an amazing friend, you may not be invited to everything. Our Tribes include individuals with a complementary variety of knowledge, skills, abilities, and personalities. When we realize that we can't be everything for anyone and encourage our friends to support each other, the Tribe benefits as a whole. Viewed this way, we should not fall victim to FOMO and instead encourage one-on-one time, even if that means our presence is not requested.

Then, of course, we can't forget about all of the cyber-bullying that happens on social media. As a mom, I find it deeply concerning that almost one in five students report being bullied during the school year and 15% report experiencing online bullying.[65] However, mean girls and bullies were not invented with the iPhone, Snapchat, and instant messaging. There is conflict online just as there is off-line. Despite that, now the harassment's potential reach and harm has expanded exponentially. We can help by practicing and teaching the golden rule not only in person, but in our newer social media frontier. Treat people as you would like to be treated and the same way online as you would in real life.

From my perspective, the next social media dilemma falls in the middle. On some occasions it may be to your bene-fit but other times, not so much. To explain my point, can you think about a time when you came across a social media acquaintance out in the real world? This is someone you may follow or who shares things of interest to you. Seeing their life on a regular basis as they choose to share it can make you feel close to that person. Closer than reality. We gain a false sense of knowing someone even though we really don't know one personal detail of their life. With this false familiarity, we may jump into conversation as if we were part of the story rather than the true observer that we are. Awkward! On the other side of the coin, being known in this way can be beneficial in some situations. If your perceived persona is a good one, your social media friends are going to feel like they know, like, and trust you before you have ever interacted one-on-one. Another reason to be an uplifter in social media!

The Good Side of Social Media

As I continued my research to find out what we know about social media and its effects on our real-life friendships, I found that along with the negative impacts, there are many positive ways that it can enhance our relationships.

For the millions of people living with social anxiety or other mental health issues, it may be much easier to converse online. The prospect of reaching out to people in person can be intimidating if not terrifying. Social media friends can be interactive without eye contact and no long-term commitment. Plus, the distance gives us time to think through what we would like to communicate versus the instant back-and-forth of an in-person conversation. Finding and connecting with like-minded individuals and groups on social media can also quickly bridge friendship gaps. The internet can serve up a perfect group of people with common interests with specificity and ease.

As I shared earlier, social media provides a great opportunity to reconnect with lost friendships. It is interesting to see how and what your high school classmates are doing now, where they live, and how much their kids look like them. My high school class has its own Facebook page, and a few times a month, I see classmates sharing information about a teacher we shared, news on another classmate, or just a fun memory or photo. It's also great for organizing reunions and activities. Recently, our class raised funds to support the charities of a classmate who experienced an untimely death. Although we have not seen each other in decades, it feels good to be a part of this community, make a difference, remember, and know that you will also be remembered.

Another positive is the speed with which we are able to communicate. We have a quick mode of communication to reach our intended audience . . . and then some. Engagement announcements, promotions, retirement, and my favorites . . . babies and puppies. Don't we all love seeing the breaking news as it happens and literally watching these life events and our kids growing up? As for our closest friendships, social media allows for us to share quickly and consistently with our BFFs. Maybe we can't get together as often as we like. To compensate, we will do whatever it takes to stay close to our friends—including connecting via social media.

But, it's important to remember that the more ways we use to connect, the stronger the bond will likely be. Here are a few habits we should foster to supplement our heavy diet of social media connection as it relates to our Tribe:

1. Pick up the phone. In today's distracted and busy culture, connecting by telephone is almost perceived as an adverse action. It should not be that way! When you can't meet up, nothing says "I care" more than a personal phone call. Voice-to-voice connection has

much more emphasis and shows you put the effort into calling them. Hearing the voice inflections, whether it be squeals of joy or tears of sorrow, are the moments that deepen the relationship.

2. Meet up in person. Are your friends a priority? If you don't prioritize your life, I promise someone else will! Set aside a lunch hour or an evening out to maintain and grow the relationships that matter to you. Put away your phone and focus on them. This will send a message that during the time you are together, they are your priority, and that feels good!

3. Check in. All too easily we can assume that *all is well* with our equally busy friendships. Show interest in what your friend is doing or what is going on in their lives. Share a dialogue, not just a "Like" on Facebook.

4. Be patient and give grace. Have you ever sent a text or left a voice message with your BFF, and she didn't get back to you as soon as you had hoped? Dumb question, right? Although the statistics I shared earlier may suggest otherwise, we aren't always glued to our cell phones. Give it some time without assuming the worst. Give your friend the benefit of the doubt and maybe a little follow-up nudge. All is well.

5. Make an effort. Don't take your friendship for granted. Friendships require attention and making an effort can really make a difference.

6. Show up and be authentic. Sometimes, life throws curve balls, and you are going to be in a position to

support a friendship in an important way. You may be at a loss as to what to say or do for your friend. Just showing up with love and demonstrating your support is enough. You will have a positive impact if you come from a good place and just BE with them.

Social media is interwoven in the social fabric of our lives. We live on the internet as much as we live in our community and neighborhoods. Considering our limited time and priorities, we should be sure to manage the time we spend on social media. It can be an open drain on our precious discretionary free time if we aren't careful. If social media is a constant temptation, think about a strategy that works for you to dive in once or twice a day for ten minutes . . . then get off. Constant connection to your phone and social media isn't good for your mental and physical health. Social media is never the prescription for staving off boredom, anxiety, or loneliness. Your family and Tribe are the remedy for that.

Remember that social media is predominantly a surface level way to connect. Every minute you spend on social media is a minute you can't use to deepen relationships. If you are like me, that is not where you generally connect with your Tribe other than liking a photo here and there and adding a comment of encouragement or love. It is a small touchpoint for our Tribe, just one more way to stay connected on a daily basis. Social media is a magnifying mirror of real life—transient but reflective. We shouldn't move away but rather recognize how it can enhance our lives, be aware of the pitfalls, and shift our focus to making the most of it. In the vast web of cyberspace, the connections that matters the most are yours.[66]

CHAPTER 10:

To Build UP or Break UP

FRIENDS COME INTO our lives for a reason, a season, or a lifetime. As we meet people, some of them capture our hearts, and some of them pass by. The ones who stick around could, with the passage of time, traverse the layers and become Tribe.

THE SEASONS OF FRIENDSHIP[67]

People come into your life for a reason, a season or a lifetime. When you figure out which one it is, you will know what to do for each person.

When someone is in your life for a REASON, it is usually to meet a need you have expressed. They have come to assist you through a difficulty; to provide you with guidance and support; to aid you physically, emotionally or spiritually. They may seem like a godsend, and they are. They are there for the reason you need them to be. Then, without any wrongdoing on your part or at an inconvenient time, this person will say or do something to bring the relationship to an end. Sometimes they die. Sometimes they walk away. Sometimes they act up and force you to take a stand. What we must realize is that our need has been met, our desire fulfilled; their work is done. The prayer you sent up has been answered and now it is time to move on.

Some people come into your life for a SEASON, because your turn has come to share, grow or learn. They bring you an experience of peace or make you laugh. They may teach you something you have never done. They usually give you an unbelievable amount of joy. Believe it. It is real. But only for a season.

LIFETIME relationships teach you lifetime lessons:

things you must build upon in order to have a solid emotional Foundation. Your job is to accept the lesson, love the person, and put what you have learned to use in all other relationships and areas of your life. It is said that love is blind, but friendship is clairvoyant.

~Author Unknown

Cut it Loose

I had a friend break up with me as a friend. She used this poem to share that I was a friend for a season. This really saddened me because I did care deeply for her. I had been surprised by something she shared with me, and I did not respond in a very kind or receptive way. I very much regret my insensitivity and wish I had reacted in a more compassionate way. I hurt her and my apologies were not going to mend the fence anytime soon. Enter stage right . . . the *"Friends for a Season"* breakup email.

At first I was a little miffed. *Really? You are going to use this platitude to tell me I'm not one of your keepers? I thought our relationship had more substance than that.* For her, it did not. I still wish things could have ended differently. After almost 20 years, I did reach out to her to say hello. We connected briefly and visited for a few minutes. I invited her to meet up sometime, to which she responded with "Sure, someday. . . ." But, nothing has ever transpired.

I get it. I have also been hurt by a few friends over the years and to me, the differences were irreconcilable. On one occasion I found the friend's comments to be so surprisingly hurtful and unfounded that I still can't think of her without reliving it. Even though she apologized almost immediately, I could not get over it. I believe that when someone shows you who they really are, you need to pay attention. If they are capable of doing or saying something that they know is hurtful, they are not only adept but likely to do it again. Hurt me once shame on you, hurt me twice shame on me.

I do not sanction my response and intolerance for arguments or enmity. At times, people make mistakes that can cause them to lash out inappropriately and uncharacteristically. By considering the context and backstory of our disagreements, we must realize that most will warrant mending and forgiveness. Perhaps I should be more tolerant. I have high expectations of myself and my friendships. Much can be pardoned; however, I do not endure disloyal and malicious or malevolent intent, no matter how brief it may be. That being said, the question must be asked: when is it time to break up with friends?

One of the largest red flags is if you realize that your friendship is primarily one-directional. Are you the one who is always reaching out, calling, and making plans? Are you on the giving side of "being there" for a friend but don't feel the gesture is returned? When you talk, is it all about her, and she rarely asks how you are doing? Friendship, like any other relationship, needs interchange in both directions in order to remain healthy. If you realize that you are doing all of the giving and your friend has been taking for years, it is time to move on.

Many times, it is through transitions in life that friendships are either forged or intimately linked. Graduations, weddings, babies, moving, and moments of great loss are all instances of clarity that spotlight relationships. These emotionally charged life events may identify friendships that have grown apart and become deadweight. You may feel like you have outgrown the friendship. On the other hand, if the friendship is moving toward Tribe, the event may actually deepen the connection.

There will be friendships that require the breakup conversation, but many of them will not. The friendship may just naturally fade away, and they will descend a layer or two in the friendship target. This indicates that there is an unspoken agreement that you are growing in different directions. You may still get together here and there, but the catch-up chat remains surface level.

When you make the decision to cut the cord on a friendship, or allow it to drift away naturally, you are sending a powerful message to the universe (and to yourself) about how you want to spend your life and energy. You also communicate what behaviors you will . . . and will not tolerate. Our time is a limited resource, and this decision will open up your calendar to build your Tribe. You are no longer investing in a dead-end relationship and can redirect your attention and nurture promising new friendships. This event is its own life transition . . . and with death comes rebirth. When a door closes, as we know, a window is opened.

Build It Up

It is natural that, as our lives change, many of our friendships will as well. However, it is not uncommon for a friendship to fade unintentionally due to simple neglect. Because we don't have any defined responsibilities in our friendships, sometimes they do not get the attention they deserve. The habitual guilt and obligation that comes with family relationships is quite the opposite with friendships. Friends are the antidote to the burdens of daily life. A daily dose of friendship can feed our mind, body, and spirit if we make time for it.

One could argue that the most powerful thing you can do to add healthy years to your life is to curate your immediate social network. Your Tribe is better than any drug or antiaging cream and will do more for you than almost any other thing. A balanced life often focuses on work and family, however, there is more to the equation. For our own wholeness, we must also account and give attention to "couplehood" with our partner, our own self-care, and our friendships. All of these elements are equally important. The good news is a good friendship can take up a lot less time than the other four components and still provide great benefits. How do we balance building our friendships with all of the other arduous roles that compete for our time? First things first. If you want to have great friendships, you must start by becoming a good friend.

Initially we can identify what relationships we would like to prioritize, the three to five friendships with whom we share similar values and a deeper connection. These are the inspiring friendships that teach and challenge you. They add joy to your life, and you can confide in them. Here we have the Enthusiasm + Vulnerability of the Tribal equation. All we need to do is add the Time + Space to = Tribe.

Here are some strategies to be a good friend:

- ***Schedule friend dates.*** Build friendship maintenance into your weekly schedule just as you would a date night with your spouse or a business meeting. These dates can be squeezed in by the hour here or there. No matter the venue—a coffee, or a cocktail—it's the time you spend with each other's full attention (phones put away) that makes the difference. It takes only a few minutes of listening and care to connect and reinforce the bonds of friendship.

- ***Focus on communication.*** Details matter. If you need to cancel a date due to a work deadline, explain the situation, so they understand what is happening in your life. Don't assume your friends can read your mind.

- ***Connect over the silly things.*** Blips of contact are the dabs of emotional glue that keep your connection solid. Share your inside jokes and funny thoughts. Think of it as your friendship drip system.

- ***Emphasize joy and kindness over charisma.*** Old and new friendships alike are enhanced when we show up with genuine enthusiasm to be with them. Kindness in your thoughts and actions demonstrates your care and appreciation. The secret to being likeable is liking other people. How you treat people does way more for a relationship than your charisma and intelligence.

- *Exercise with friends.* This is something you should be doing anyway! You can kill two birds with one stone: self-care and girl time. Experiencing things together strengthens your bonds, builds history, and adds to your story.

- *Tell her you love her.* We just don't share our feelings and let people know often enough what they mean to us. Don't wait! If it feels awkward at first, it will get easier, I promise.

- *Give gifts from afar.* When my parents traveled, we kids were always excited for their return, not only because we missed them, but because of the suitcase surprise. We could always count on a gift of some small souvenir from their trip. In a similar spirit, when you return from travel and give your friend a small trinket from your trip, it lets them know you were thinking about them.

- *Text or tag them in a photo.* See something that reminds you of your friend? Snap a photo and send it to them. It takes less than a minute to do so, and the thoughtfulness will not go unnoticed.

- *Drop by for a hug.* Driving by your friend's office? Pop in for a quick hello and squeeze. It will uplift you both and give you each a natural dose of oxytocin.

- *Pick up the phone.* Your voice on the other end of the line is more powerful than any text. Vocal tone accounts for a significant percentage of communication about feelings. Texts, emails, and DMs are like emotional cliff notes—they give an outline of the story but not the full sentiment behind it. On the phone you can hear your friend's unguarded thoughts, pauses, and sighs.

- **Share an inspirational quote or funny meme.** If something strikes you as funny or moving, share it with a friend via social media, email, or text. Just another *drop* in the friendship drip system.

- **Show up.** Nothing says you care like being there, whether it be traveling to a wedding, showing up at a kid's graduation, or attending a grandparent's memorial service. Being a part of important life moments is a strong signal that you are there for your friends. Real friends are present even during challenging situations. Be there, even if it is just sitting together in silence.

- **Break bread.** Sharing a meal touches all of our senses: sight, touch, taste, smell, and hearing. Conversation takes place and our bonds and feelings of well-being increase. Food + Friendships = FUN!

- **Share a theme song.** Find a song that reminds you of your friend. Maybe you first heard it together at a dance club, or the lyrics remind you of them in some way. Music helps foster deeper social connections. It is said that listening to music activates many areas of the brain, including the part that helps us connect with what others are thinking and feeling.

- **Be vulnerable.** Sharing your true feelings and asking for support makes friendships stronger. You may feel like asking for help would burden your friends, but that is not the case. Your friends want to be of service and especially to their BFFs.

- **Offer specific support.** You can see that your friend is going through something. Don't just say, "Can I help you?" or "Let me know what I can do." Offer specific support like, "Can I bring over a lasagna to feed the kids tonight?" or "Can I run to the Chinese Restaurant and pick up your favorite Egg Drop Soup since you aren't feeling well?" It's very hard for people to ask for help. You want to make it as easy as possible for them to accept your help.

- **Consistency matters more than frequency.** Create your own monthly and yearly traditions. Our girlfriends have a standing date on the third Thursday of every month for *Women Who Wine*. Even when schedules get crazy, we can count on that one night to connect! Can't commit to monthly? Really good friendships have an emotional longevity that makes them resilient to dormant periods. One friend suggested that we have a standing date on Flag Day. When our lives got so busy with our kids and careers, this mostly uncelebrated date became our excuse and reminder to get together, and it didn't compete with traditional family holidays.

What fun rituals we can begin creating with our friendships! Adding just one or two of the ideas above could impact your relationship in a short time period. Logging these hours as a labor of love and scheduling time with your closest friends will surely pay off. If you are interested in receiving a new idea each week for fun ways to deepen your friendships, visit the www.LadyAndTheTribe.com and find the subscribe button. Let's talk more about how we can be a good friend to our besties.

You are Perfectly Imperfect

One important quality we expect from our best friends is authenticity: just being real. If we are constantly trying to be someone we are not, to impress, or to fit in, we are not attracting the friendships that will become Tribe. Generally speaking, people will figure out this facade quickly. It is a turnoff. We are most attracted (platonically) to others who are comfortable in their own skin. Real friendships are relaxed around each other. Even in complete silence, great friends can enjoy each other's company just *being* together. The way you handle your strengths and weaknesses with humility and confidence will give your friends permission to be real and relaxed with you as well. Perfection is overrated. Be yourself!

Sense and Sensitivity

Have you ever had the feeling that something was wrong or *off* with a friend? If you want to show you care, check in on her and make sure she is okay. Call, text, or better yet, stop by in person. Without going overboard, let her know that you are concerned and want to help or just listen. Make an excuse to spend time with her. If she opens up to you, be mindful not to immediately start sharing your opinions or giving your advice unless you are asked for it. Listen to her. Acknowledge and validate her feelings and offer encouragement. Being heard, seen, and understood is an affirming gift that can mean the world.

The Hard Truth

Do these jeans make my butt look big? Now ladies, as we know, the truth hurts sometimes. There is a point where you just don't want to hurt your friend's feelings, *butt* it's time for a friendly intervention. True friends will tell each other the truth even when it is hard. We can avoid the brutal part of honesty when it is necessary by offering constructive advice from a place of love. Let her know you care about her. Honesty is such an important foundational element of Tribal friendships.

Perhaps your friend has developed a bad habit, or you see them going down the wrong path. Offer your assistance in kicking the habit or making a detour. Maybe they are drinking or smoking too much. Because you care, you could kindly point it out and share that you are concerned for them. Perhaps it is something as minor as a bad case of halitosis or a piece of pepper in their teeth before date night. Nobody loves being the bearer of this news, but as a BFF, that is your job and what you would hope for in return. Set her up for success with a kind FYI so she can correct the situation and have a stellar date!

Furthermore, keep your promises and do what you say you are going to do. It's as simple as that. Lies, white lies, and half-truths almost always end up surfacing and can destroy trust.

In the Bible King Solomon said, "Faithful are the wounds of a friend, but the kisses of an enemy are deceitful."[68] If you value your friendship, always be constructively honest even when it is uncomfortable.

Brief but Undivided Moments

Your time with your friendships is limited, so it is important that you give them your full attention. Take interest in the details of their life and be an active listener. By knowing and understanding some of the finer details of their lives you can become part of the story, which will further deepen your connection. What are they most excited about right now? What are they looking forward to? What is keeping them up at night? Caring enough to ask and listening to understand her point of view is a huge gift, providing a foundation of acceptance. She will return to this safety zone, you, her confidante, as she needs support or to share a victory.

Your treasured one-on-one date is a time to put your phone away and *be there*. The present moment is a gift to yourself and your friendships. Don't ruin it by answering texts or emails and scrolling through your Facebook feed. We are so addicted to these bad habits that it will probably be challenging at first. It will feel like you are missing or forgetting something. Avoid the temptation to dig it out of your purse and take a peek. It will get easier. Maybe your friend is the one who is tied to her technology. You could kindly suggest that when together, you create a ritual of keeping your phones off the table and out of arm's reach to limit distractions. It is a simple respect you can show each other. Soon you will look forward to this vacation from the noise that allows for a deep dive into your girl time.

Keeper of Secrets

Secrets. Aren't they a double-edged sword? On one hand, you are delighted and honored that someone trusts you enough to confide in you a secret. On the other hand, this responsibility is quite a burden! It makes no difference if the information is exciting, shocking, personal, big, or small, you are now under obligation to keep your lips sealed. If you betray that trust, at a minimum it could be destructive to your friendship and prevent it from growing deeper. It is possible you could damage the relationship beyond repair, effectively ending the friendship. Your own reputation could take a hit, you will become "someone not to be trusted" when the word gets out.

Rather than immediately leaning in with an interested *do tell* when you hear, "I have a secret," you may want to take a step back. Accepting the responsibility of a secret can be a life changing decision. When it comes to your Tribe, you are building lifelong friendships with these ladies. You don't want to jeopardize this relationship if you are a bad secret keeper. You know who you are! You may want to consider asking a few follow-up questions prior to consenting to hear a secret. For example, when someone says they have a secret to share you may want to ask:

1. Is it a big secret or a little secret?
2. How long must I keep this secret?

3. Ask if there is anyone else who knows or anyone you are allowed to tell.

Knowing the answers to these questions will help you decide if you can handle, or even want, the responsibility. If you only have to keep the secret a certain amount of time instead of *forever*, that is good to know up front. If you know you will tell someone, like your spouse, be up front with that disclosure as well. If you don't think you can handle the pressure of a secret, stop them before they tell you. As exciting as having a secret is, keeping a secret can be stressful. As a general rule, if you like to avoid stress, just say no to secrets.

On the other hand, what are best friends for if you can't share a secret? As we grow in vulnerability and depth with our Tribe, there are bound to be conversations that include sensitive topics and require confidentiality. The secret keeping skill is a must have for Tribe, so if you have trouble in this area, it is a skill you should develop. If you have a secret to keep, here are a few suggestions that may help you be a better secret keeper:[69]

1. Avoid the topic. Even related topics should be evaded as they are the *gateway drug* to consciously or unconsciously oversharing and accidently spilling the beans.
2. Change the topic. Is the discussion getting too close for comfort to the secret? Casually steer the conversation in a different direction entirely.
3. Remove yourself from the conversation. Sometimes this is your only escape. Find an excuse to leave.

4. Become a deer in the headlights. If someone asks you a direct question about the secret, pretend you don't know anything about it. One could say that this is borderline *lying*, so it should only be done as a last resort.

5. Honest avoidance. If you are pressed for information, tell them that it isn't something you can talk about at this time. Ask them not to question you about it anymore.

When is it necessary to tell a secret? Does the secret endanger someone? Does it involve them harming themselves or someone else? Is it criminal? These are all things to consider when determining if the secret is too important to keep. There is a point when NOT keeping their secret is to their ultimate benefit. It's a tough spot to be in and the decision may be hard, but it is a small price to pay to be a good friend.

A Dangerous Secret

Pam:

I had just witnessed my intoxicated husband get into a fistfight with my son who heard me screaming from his room in the basement. We had been arguing, and my husband had pinned me on the couch. My son pulled him off of me and began fighting him. I couldn't watch. I had to look away.

This man who I had fallen deeply in love with only a few short years ago had become a bully and tyrant in my life. What had been limited to verbal abuse over the past year just crossed over to the physical. How did I not see this coming?

My son gained the advantage and threw HIM outside then looked at me. Having heard some of the verbal abuse I had been the recipient of in the past, my son sternly gave me a directive, "Stay with family, a friend, or anywhere; just get away from HIM." I called Krista, one of my Tribe members, who knew HIM well. I was scared, upset, and also embarrassed. Why had I tolerated this so long? I knew my dear friend would be there for me, listen to my worries, and support me. I was in a dark place and in confidence, I vocalized some of the crazy solutions that were running through my mind.

Krista:
The night Pam came to my house, I had just returned to work after maternity leave from having my twins. I felt my hair was on fire already, but my friend needed me, so the world stopped. The look on her face was one of total heartbreak. Behind closed doors, we her Tribe, knew something had been off with her marriage. We were worried for her but did not realize how bad it had gotten.

With bruises on her arm, puffy eyes, and tears still flowing, she showed up on my doorstep. Her secret was out. Pam knew now there was no turning back, or she could lose her son's relationship. I watched her struggle with heartache, loss, and uncertainty and tried to comfort her. I was glad Pam was here, safe with me.

Pam began saying things that brought me great distress. She said things like "Krista, sometimes I think it would be better if I was just dead. People would be better off without me. I could take pills and just not wake up the next day." Pam would follow up by halfheartedly suggesting she wasn't serious, but I'd been through this before. When someone feels like they are a burden on everyone, and expresses it, that is a sign that suicide is on the table. Secrets are for best friends, but this one was just too big to keep to myself.

Pam:
Krista didn't like me blaming myself, and I turned down a dark path of potentially doing something stupid. She then decided to tell the rest of the Tribe without my knowledge or permission. She asked them to check on me, telling them I was not okay. I felt betrayed by Krista and very embarrassed. I was ashamed of staying with him, putting up with his abuse, and now everyone knew.

Krista:
Floundering as to what she should do next, Pam stayed with me. Over the days to follow, crisis and ultimatums turned into HIS apologies and promises to do better and be better. Against the vigorous pleading of her friends and family, Pam returned home.

"Leave us alone," was HIS demand, "so we can fix us." Pam became isolated. It was killing her. I reached out to HIM and asked if he would talk to me since we had also been friends. I saw that he was deep in alcoholism and dragging my best friend down with him. I asked him to go to counseling or get help with his drinking. He blamed it all on Pam and said, "She's the one who needs the help." He was gaslighting her and trying to sell that story to me. I told him "You're going to lose everything!" He didn't care. He would rather have the alcohol than Pam and his family.

This was a really tough time. Pam was very angry with me for what seemed a very long time. I feel like she blamed me for having to choose between HIM and her family. For a time, I was the scapegoat and Pam ostracized me for my involvement. I don't regret telling the Tribe. Pam needed us . . . all of us. I feel the girls were helpful and supportive to Pam, and when they did get involved, they were attentive, encouraging, and respectful.

Pam:

When I went back, my son had moved out and my daughter would not let the grandkids come over. I lived like this for another six months. The family did not include HIM for the holidays or events. Things were still rocky with his drinking, calling me names and bullying, but nothing physical. Our anniversary was upon us, and I was looking forward to traveling with HIM and working on our marriage. We were going to Thailand! We had reserved a tour where every detail was taken care of. I had always wanted to go ... to travel all over the world ... with my husband. I was so excited.

Two hours before leaving ... at the airport ... he told me he was not going. He said he didn't want to go with me and fight all week. He dropped me and my things and left me on the curb. I was frantic. I couldn't believe what had just happened to me! What do I do? Who do I call? Krista.

Krista told me "Get your ass on that plane! Cry if you need to but get on that plane! If you need to come home, we will figure that out, just get on the plane! You can do this!"

Krista:

I will never forget that. They had been contemplating .. . to go or not to go. It wasn't until they got to the airport that he said he wasn't going. What a jerk! I asked Pam, "Do you want to go to Thailand?" Pam said "Yes!" I told her, "Then get on that plane!" She was sobbing hysterically. I stayed on the phone with her as she went through security, had a preflight drink at a lounge and all the way to the gate. She called me on her layover at 3:00 a.m.! I encouraged her all the way that she can do hard things.

Pam:

Krista told me, "Go get a massage, go on a tour, and see the sights!" Still on an emotional roller coaster, the tour kept me busy with a packed agenda, and I enjoyed making new friends with the other passengers. The trip was both mentally and physically challenging but also life changing and spiritual. I was growing all the way, alone but not alone. Krista walked me through it every day. With my Tribe's encouragement, text messages, Marco Polo video messages, and endless support, simply being there yet far, far away. I was broken, but my AMAZING WOMEN who knew me best truly accompanied me on my solo trip to Thailand. That was the beginning of a new journey for me. A new life. Today I feel like I've found my way back to me and couldn't be happier. I couldn't have done it without Krista and my Tribe.

Krista:

Pam came back from Thailand and realized she could do anything . . . all by herself. I'm so proud of her. She had to start building a life of her own without HIM, or I feared she would never leave. She did it. She is happy again, and I have my free spirit, life of the party, loving Pam back.

Misunderstandings and Allegiance

Most people will do almost anything to avoid a clash. To be honest, I don't love conflict either. However, I much prefer it to stewing on the details of an issue for days, weeks, or months. In the past, I have been guilty of lying in bed, revisiting a transgression and imagining what I woulda-coulda-shoulda done at the time. I would imagine a backstory of all kinds of sinister motives the other party may have had. What a terrible waste of time that was! All it takes is five seconds of courage to pick up the phone and say, "Hey Julie, when this happened the other day, this is the way it made me feel." I have found that often "Julie" had no idea there was an issue, and she certainly had no intention of hurting me.

Having learned this lesson years ago, I choose to initiate those difficult conversations to relieve myself of unnecessary hard feelings and to protect the friendship. I have high expectations of my close friendships and anticipate that they respect our relationship enough to do the same. I see this level of communication as an act of loyalty.

Most likely, all of us have experienced lack of communication or misunderstandings in situations like this. There have been a few relationships in my life that, after years of history and bonding, they ended abruptly due to lack of communication and/or loyalty. When this has happened, it is always a surprise because I just don't see it coming. It usually occurs when the *friend* doesn't have the courage to communicate something that is bothering them. Unaddressed, these issues can only build upon themselves with assumptions and ill will. Eventually they erupt, blindsiding the friendship, and the relationship can never be the same again. Yes, I am speaking from experience.

As I stated before, we aren't all wired the same. Statistically speaking, most people are averse to confrontational situations, and that is okay... it's expected. On occasion, the kindest thing you can do for your friendship is to face off and put a voice to your pain. Think of it this way: how would it make you feel if a friend connected privately and shared in a sincere way that her feelings had been hurt by you or that she didn't like something you did? At first you will probably feel a little defensive—but take a breath and really listen. She is giving you the opportunity to see things from her perspective so that you may share yours. You are receiving a precious moment of vulnerability and a chance to set the record straight. Your relationship means enough to her to initiate this hard conversation. When you think of it this way, isn't this hard conversation a gift?

Loyalty is unconditional acceptance. Even when you mess up, the friendship advocates for your best interests. When someone is gossiping or attacking you behind your back, your true friend shields you and stands for you. When you have unintentionally done something to offend, your friend will communicate their feelings. They do this because they love you, value you, and care about your relationship.

Practice giving the gift of open communication. You can foster this Tribe culture by establishing an up-front contract on how you will handle misunderstandings when they arise. This pre-conflict conversation will set the tone and encourage addressing things before they get out of hand. Just as you may set *fair fighting rules* with your spouse when it comes to disagreements, you can create rules of engagement as it pertains to conflict with your Tribe. You are giving each other permission to be vulnerable, speak up when something is upsetting, and promise to listen attentively with an open heart. Be loyal to your friendships and reciprocity will do the rest.

CHAPTER 11:

Finding Friends

HOW DO WE make new friends—especially with the impact of social distancing? It starts with *intention* and ends with *action*. We must be intentional about connecting to others because it may not happen naturally. So, let's start from here as if we are inspired for the very first time to build our own Tribe. Maybe you have a bunch of contacts on Facebook and haven't really known what you were missing . . . until now. Perhaps your life has been so full as a wife and mother you have made little time for anything else . . . until now. Possibly your career has had you on the run from dawn until dusk for a decade, and you just hadn't created the space for deep friendship . . . until now. All it takes is a decision, a plan, and then action on your part to make it happen.

New Tribe in Town

Traci's Story:

When I was married, I invested every waking moment with my kids. My husband was away a lot, so I just went to work and then came home almost every day. I didn't really have any friends. At one point I joined a boot camp exercise group, so I did meet a few women. That was the first thing I started doing for myself. Even then, I struggled with mom guilt. *Should I really be doing this? Spending time and money on myself?* But I did find it made me happy.

It wasn't until becoming single again and moving to Manhattan, Kansas, that I started focusing more on my own friendships. It was a big adjustment for us because the kids were used to me always being home. Prior to this, I took them with me everywhere. I never did anything without them. If I did need to leave them for a while, the kids would cry and throw a fit, and I would feel awful.

My kids had some great friends, and through them, I met some great mothers. One pulled me in and included me in her Tribe's girls night events. Another couple of ladies joined a workout group with me. This new group of women were very supportive and encouraged me: "You need this time with your friends. It is okay; you will be a better mom for taking this time for yourself." This foursome was a pretty established friend group and really great about doing things together. I was amazed . . . they introduced me to this whole new world of camaraderie I hadn't experienced before. These women get together, go out, hang out, have fun, and sometimes just "be" together? Wow!

Early on, when I would get invited to gatherings, I decided, *I'm going to make EVERY effort to go because if I say no a few times, they will think I am not interested and might stop inviting.* I knew a couple of the ladies better than the rest. When they couldn't go for some reason, I still made a point to show up so that they knew I was interested in spending time with all of them. This also helped me bond with the rest of the women.

I was drawn to these ladies because they knew how to have fun. It was the kind of fun that I was looking for. Not a big production. Sometimes we just hung out at someone's house. I felt it was a judgment-free zone.

I'm still a part of this Tribe today. I've learned that I am definitely one of those people who need this connection. With all of the roles I play as a woman, a mother, and a professional, I am constantly giving. The time I spend with these women fills me back up, so I can go out and give another day!

I just love our girls' trips where we can just relax, take a breath, and be silly girls. Once, we danced the night away, which we don't usually do. But in the weekend getaway environment, we just felt so free. It was a blast.

The relationships I have built within the Tribe are incredibly supportive. When I decided to end a long-term dating relationship, my best friend was there to just listen and offer encouragement. Sometimes I felt like I was talking a lot. I didn't want to be like, "Me, me, me, me . . . it's all about me." I told her "I'm sure you are just sick of hearing about this!" She said, "No I'm not. Tell me how you are feeling." Sometimes you need to vent, be heard, and ask for guidance, trusting that your friendship has your best interests at heart. She was really there for me. Present. I am grateful.

Now when the kids ask why I am going out or away for a quick weekend, I tell them, "I am a better mom when I get to spend some time with my friends." At the same time, I hope that I am modeling for them how to take care of themselves. I think many women don't realize what they are missing. I was right there before I met this group of women.

My advice if you feel you are lacking deep friendship? As scary as it is, try to put yourself out there. Make it a priority. What are the things that make you happy? Do those things, and you will find others who also enjoy those things. Soon you will find other things in common.

We are no longer simply friends of convenience because of our kids. We have forged past the friendlies zone so that our friendships stand alone. My Tribe is the best thing that has happened to me in Manhattan. I hope that they truly know and understand how very important they are to me. They are what keeps me sane. We have fun, take time to be silly, talk, and be real. My Tribe truly gets me through most days. They are an awesome group of women, and I feel very lucky. I tell everyone, "I'm not great at picking men, but I am great at picking friends. I nailed it in the friend category."

Traci was at a point in her life where she recognized that she needed this group of women. She stepped out of her comfort zone, got off the couch even when it was calling her to stay, and made the effort to connect. The bounties of taking a chance have been life changing.

Decision Day

Not making a decision . . . is a decision. Every day we make decisions moment by moment on things ranging from the inconsequential to the life altering. The fact is that your day, year, and entire life are defined by the sum of the decisions you make and the actions you take along the way. Everything you have experienced, both the good and the bad, started with a decision and has shaped your life.

Indecision is a decision by default. In this position, you are no longer in the driver's seat. You let chance, fate, or others direct your future. How many times have you allowed life to happen *to you* instead of directing the outcome? To some extent, we all may suffer from decision paralysis at some point in time. The decisions you are making every day or are allowing to be made on your behalf will determine how you feel today and who you are tomorrow. When you hold yourself to a higher standard you take control instead of letting conditions take control of you.

Today is the Day

Do you want to build a Tribe of deep, meaningful, lifelong friendships? Maybe you already have a best friend and/or pack of besties but want to take it to the next level. How do you want your Tribe and friendships to look 90 days from today? How about six months, one year, and five years from now? The small adjustments and friendship habits you decide on and implement today will determine the future of your Tribe. Decide on a new friendship goal. When you identify the desired outcome, it sets universal forces in motion. The universe has your back and will begin to line up the path and assist you in reaching your goal.

Begin the process with a little brainstorming session. Daydream for a few moments about what your life will look like once you have established and nurtured your Tribe. How will it make you feel to have a steadfast cheering section that will encourage you and celebrate every little victory in your life? You now have someone to turn to when you need honest advice. You feel secure in that your secrets can be shared, yet you are confident that they are safe and in good hands. You share meaningful bonding experiences filled with fun and adventure. You connect regularly, and you leave each encounter filled to the brim with love, acceptance, and validation. You feel unstoppable because with your Tribe's support, you can overcome any obstacle and reach every goal. You have a pack to run with through life. That is the power of your future Tribe.

Close your eyes and picture in your mind these foundational friendships in action. See their smiling faces beam when you walk in the door. Feel the joy you receive with their loving hugs and squeezes. See it so clearly that you feel as if you are there right now. This exercise is quite motivating and allows you to feel a sense of the benefits you will receive before the goal is accomplished. Visualization is a powerful tool that accelerates the universe's energies toward actualizing your intention. Whatever you can dream, see, and believe in your mind, you can achieve.

Now put it on paper. Journal your future life story; write as if it has already happened. Write about your Tribe and how it has impacted your life. How many members are in your Tribe? Write about each kind of friendship you are seeking and how each individual adds value to your Tribe. How do you support each other? What kinds of activities do you enjoy doing together? How do you connect on a regular basis? How do you feel now that you have this group of women who always have your back? Write down your gratitude for having such a perfectly imperfect Tribe. As you write each sentence, go to that feeling place and activate the joy, gratitude, and peace that are sure to come with this new powerful part of your life.

There is magic in writing down our vision. Putting our desires, hopes, and dreams actualized down on paper helps them become real. This method and action of writing down our goals brings clarity and focus to what we really want. It cements our ideas and takes those floating dreams from our head and heart and brings them into the present here and now. Seeing it in writing makes it suddenly feel real and gives us that sense of possibility.

Close your eyes and imagine your declared dream and feel the emotions as if you have achieved the moment. This exercise is a powerful step in the creation process. You now know what you want your Tribe to be and can see it clearly. The feeling you practiced generates a universal path that leads you to your dream actualized. We can spend all day wishing things were different or a fraction of that time making a plan and setting it into motion. You have made the decision. Now go after it.

The Plan

How will you connect with new women who could become future Tribe members? What existing friendships would you like to nurture into Tribe? What specific habits can you establish to deepen the connections of your current Tribe? The sky's the limit here—get creative! Here are dozens of examples of friendship habits you may consider building into your routine:

Networking for new blood:

1. Get out of the house! You aren't going to meet anyone binge watching Netflix!

2. Challenge yourself to put your phone away when you are out in public. Instead find opportunities to make conversation. When you are on the go and focused on your phone as you wait in lines, or even as you are walking, you miss a lot of connection possibilities. Your routine likely takes you past some of the same people every day. If you say hello or chat for a few minutes, that is a breeding ground for friendship. You miss these opportunities with your nose buried in the phone.

3. Sign up for a class: Spanish, Zumba, art, cooking, baking, bird watching, wine tasting, or whatever! What are you interested in? Here you will meet others who have the same interests. Give it a chance. Commit to attending a minimum of three classes. Once you have made a few contacts, just keep showing up!

4. Open up a conversation with a stranger. Use the *insight and question method*. This conversation starter involves commenting on current events, then asking a question about their opinion of it. Research has shown that expressing our opinions activates brain regions that are associated with pleasure and reward. Your question will likely be received with gratitude for the opportunity to share. Steer clear of hot divisive topics. You are inviting conversation, not debate.

5. Volunteer for a good cause and connection. Build a house for the homeless, serve a meal to the hungry, or clean up a park to beautify the neighborhood. You will meet some great people who also care about the community. Strike up a conversation with someone and reconnect each time you volunteer together.

6. Join a club. There are all kinds of clubs out there. Seek one that interests you! Running, walking, hiking, beer/wine tasting, travel, dining, paddle boarding, sailing, golf, and community service just to name a few! You already have something in common to talk about with these folks, so making new friends will be easy! Let friendship be a result of doing something you enjoy.

7. Be a good listener. You have one mouth and two ears. Practice using them accordingly. Don't dominate the conversation. If you want more friends, ask people about themselves and listen sincerely when they answer. Listen not to respond but to understand. A good listener is rare these days. It is the best direct route

ticket you could possibly have to form a friendship.

8. Find a local online group that discusses topics of interest to you. Actively participate in the discussions and meet up with them when they have an activity. If they don't ever get together, suggest that they do so!

9. Tap into your "friends of friends" network. Take an inventory of who you know and who *they* know. This may be someone you have seen around but had yet to be introduced. Exploring adjacent friends gives you a head start in the connection process because you already have a friend in common.

10. Start a meetup involving one of your interests. Meetup. com is great place to easily start your own group, or search the site for already established groups.

Nurturing to the next level:

1. Start a book club that convenes every couple of weeks. Invite friends and ask them to reach out to *their* friends and begin to bring new people into the fold.

2. Welcome newcomers and include others. Give the gift of inclusivity and belonging to a potential new Tribe member. Sit beside someone you don't know well rather than always sitting with existing friends.

3. Intentionally connect deeper with Hi/Bye friends or acquaintances. These are the folks you say hi to when you see them and bye at the end of the day, but that's about it.

4. Invite an interesting acquaintance to lunch or coffee. Show interest in them beyond surface level niceties.

5. Make an effort with coworkers. Start by grabbing lunch with them once a week. You will become closer over time and connect in a more meaningful way. Get rid of any notions you have of separating your social life from your professional life.

6. Ask good questions that draw others into meaningful conversations. Share a personal story. Real stories draw people together.

7. Connect with authenticity. Have you ever caught yourself thinking about what you will say next as someone you are visiting with is talking? Often we are too caught up with our own concerns: "What does she think of me? What should I say or do next?" We not only miss the point she is making *but* the entire point of working on friendship.

8. Book a meeting from a meeting. Keep in mind that the consistency of exposures goes further to build a relationship than the connection does alone. You need at least three exposures to establish a friendship and determine if they are a Tribe candidate. When you are meeting for coffee, don't leave without setting another friendship date. Don't spread the dates out too far. Doing so will just prolong the courtship, and appointments set too far in advance are more likely to be rescheduled or missed all together.

9. Become a regular. There is a social power to simply showing up and being present. Becoming a fixture of

sorts in a setting creates repeated interaction opportunities and launches the *mere exposure effect*. This phenomenon has been studied and shows that we tend to like things in direct proportion to how familiar they seem.

10. Start saying "YES" to your neighbor's Christmas party or happy hour after work with coworkers. Accept invites you receive to socialize. Get out there!

Intensify building history, connection, and depth:

1. Once a week, invite a Tribe member to do something together: a yoga class, brunch, a hike, or a cup of coffee or tea on the back porch.

2. Set a monthly standing date, something like the third Thursday of each month for a Kindred Clan get together. This could be anything from game night to Bunco to a potluck to karaoke! My Tribe's circles (Kindred Clan) meet up for Women Who Wine Happy Hour every month. It is always fun to see who shows up and how the connections evolve.

3. Find a reason to celebrate! Every month look for an excuse to get the Tribe together: birthdays, holidays, the first day of summer—or just make up something!

4. Share a giggle. When something strikes you as funny, share it with one or more ladies in your Tribe. Send a text, a video message, or better yet, a quick phone call.

5. Take out your weekly/monthly calendar and block out time for Tribe. Even if you don't have anything specific

to schedule, block the time and set a friendship date. Being intentional will create space, so your Tribe-time isn't crowded out.

6. Show up. How can you support a friend this week or month? Go watch them win a tennis tournament. Help them get their patio ready for summer. Take them to lunch while their car is getting an oil change. Sit with them in the waiting room before a wellness visit. Suggest a walking date when they are trying to add some healthy habits.

7. Be real and go deep. Commit to yourself that when you need support or someone to listen, you will reach out and ask for help. Be brave about sharing your needs and struggles when appropriate. Vulnerability is like cement between the bricks of friendship.

8. Send a letter or card to a Tribe member and share something specific that you appreciate about them and their friendship. Texts are great, but there is something special about getting a letter or note you can hold and keep. Besides, isn't it a nice surprise to get something other than bills in the mail?

9. Plan a Tribe adventure, something to look forward to. Can you say road trip? How about a night out in the Big City? Sign up for a personal growth seminar. Skydiving anyone? Train together for a half marathon or mud run. These history building activities will be something exciting to look forward to and become memories you will look back on and cherish.

10. Something old, something new, something borrowed, something blue.

   a. Share an *old favorite: a* movie, restaurant, club, or picnic spot as an excuse to hang out.

   b. Dying to try something new? A dance class, a new wine bar, or a new comedy show are all fun experiences to share.

   c. Lend her your favorite book or shawl. This meaningful gesture communicates love and trust.

   d. Feeling blue? Hard times hit us all, and sharing the experience and being there for each other deepens our bond.

For new weekly ideas on ways to connect and build Tribe, sign up for my weekly newsletter www.LadyAndTheTribe.com.

Fast Friendship

Adriana had just a few friends when she moved to Colorado. None of them live in the state, and one lives outside the country. She explains that she has had other friendships along the way that, for one reason or another, just didn't work out. "I had a couple of close friends in graduate school, and when I was getting married, they completely disconnected from me. I was mortified," Adriana remembers.

At the time she was also mourning the loss of her relationship with her mother and could have really used the support. After all that drama, she decided that it was time to focus on her child and career. She just didn't have the time to cultivate girlfriends. After her last experience, why go there anyway? Newly remarried, she was running head down and focused only on her family and career.

Just six short months ago, a pageant friend connected with her in an instant message. She said, "Hey girl, I know of someone you would get along fabulously with. She's into dogs just like you. Her name is Jamie, and I would love to connect you." Adriana agreed to the connection. Why not?

Adriana and Jamie started with small chitchat on messenger and then very soon Jamie asked, "What are you doing tomorrow? Why don't you come over to my house?" Adriana felt a bit unsettled and surprised by the proposition. "I was like . . . okay . . ." Adriana admits.

Jamie didn't think this was weird at all. She declares, "I was born and raised in Texas, and that is what we do." She teases, "It's that southern hospitality that apparently you Coloradans don't know about."

Adriana pulled up to Jamie's address and texted her husband to let him know she was there . . . just in case. "I planned on hanging out for maybe two hours, but I ended up being there for five hours! I was blown away by her generosity and the ease in which we hit it off."

A personal trainer by trade, Adriana started training with Jamie each week. Jamie immediately started inviting her to social events and get-togethers. "I was not used to this because my best friends are all over the planet: one in Italy, one in Tampa, and another in Louisville." Adriana shares, "I have had a hard time connecting with women here in Colorado because the impression I get is that women here are just on the go, moving and shaking, and the opportunities to connect are not plentiful. Everyone is busy. I was not used to building deep connections with friends and then Jamie comes along and knocks my socks off. I was like 'You don't know me . . . why are you so open and inviting?'"

Adriana started going to Jamie's girl's events and having a lot of fun. Jamie would have gifts for everyone. At one point, Adriana became overwhelmed with emotion at her generosity to the point of tears. Jamie kidded, "We have a crier!" Jamie explained that she grew up with nothing. "Many people along the way helped me, so now, I want to be giving and help others as much as I can."

Shortly into their friendship, Jamie's mom needed to move from Texas to Colorado, and it was happening fast. Jamie told Adriana about her upcoming trip and that she planned on going alone. Adriana asked, "How long is this trip? By yourself??" Nope! There was no way she could do this by herself, Moves are taxing on everyone, let alone Jamie who had just had hip surgery two months prior! Adriana asked, "Need someone to go with you?" Jaime replied, "Please?" After knowing Jamie for less than two months, Adriana cleared her schedule and went with her.

In appreciation and disbelief, Jamie shares, "I don't know why Adriana puts me on a pedestal. I don't understand why she feels I have done so much for her. I feel like it is the other way around, and she has done so much for me. When Adriana walked into my life, I was a mess."

Jamie had been recovering from hip surgery and struggling with thyroid problems and other medical issues that had her doctors prescribing a myriad of medications. These meds were not only affecting her body but her mind and spirit—all in a negative way. One day during a personal training session with Adriana, Jamie suddenly threw the weights across the room and flipped out. Shocked, Adriana said, "Whoa-hey.. . alright! We are going outside! Let's go, let's go!" Jamie unleashed all of her frustrations about how no one understood what was happening to her and all that she was going through. "Something is wrong. I know my body; this isn't right. I can't even function day-to-day." After this breakdown and many tests, Jamie discovered that the meds were contraindicated and killing her little by little every day. She dumped almost all of them down the drain. She is still on the mend and finally feeling an upswing.

Adriana shares, "Since meeting Jamie, I have had many super-fast life lessons come into the picture. I have been reminded of the stuff that matters most." Jamie has been instrumental in helping Adriana cope with her husband's recent diagnosis of lymphoma. When she got the news, she was both anxious to tell Jamie, and at the same time, dreaded telling her. Jamie, having been through it herself has been a supportive resource. "So many dimensions of life have happened in the short time since I met Jamie."

Crying, Adriana addresses Jamie across the table, "Look at you . . . I appreciate you! How can words convey what our friendship means to me . . . dare I say, I love you? You have made such an impact in my life. I get very protective of you and defensive for you because this kind of connection doesn't just happen." Adriana began with some walls up around women and friendship. Jamie's kindness and inclusivity broke her open.

In turn, Adriana was called to help Jamie, physically as well as mentally.

"Life can be cruel, but it is always beautiful . . . possibility mixed with complications". Adriana admits, "I could have continued in fear and said, 'I don't want to get hurt so I'm not going to be vulnerable.' I would have missed out on this incredible friendship that has impacted my life so greatly. Yes, we have known each other for a short amount of time, but there is nothing I wouldn't do for her. I cherish this friendship."

In your journal, create a plan that supports the decision you made to build your Tribe. Pick out three to five actions from the lists above—or ones that you come up with on your own. Make a commitment to yourself to put your plan into action after writing it down.

Lao Tzu (6th century BC), a Chinese philosopher speaks of a very long journey beginning with only a single step.[70] Although literally true, I don't believe Tzu was referring to a physical journey but rather a decision. The first step is never physical. It is entirely mental. The first step is a decision. A decision to commit. A decision to act. Decision also means cutting off, division, or detachment of a part.[71] It's as if by making a decision, we are eliminating all other options. People who are decisive show confidence in character and purpose. Those are strong descriptive words that we can aspire to and accomplish by making a decision to act.[71]

The minute you make a decision, you have set your life in a new direction. It is exciting to think that you have the power to change your trajectory on anything in an instant. If your relationships aren't where you want them to be, you don't need to continue telling that story. Having made the decision to build your Tribe and vowing to accept no other outcome, you now have a new story. It is time to put your decision to work.

Action

Commit to your decision by taking action. Stating the goal or the decision is not enough. Does this goal scare you a little? Yes? Good! You are leaving your comfort zone and are about to create some new habits that will serve you. This may be a bit scary but also exciting! You may not know each step you will take, and that may cause some anxiety. Fear prevents many people from taking action. You don't need to plan out every possible detail to build your Tribe. You will find your way, one step at a time. Your journey, however, will begin with a single step toward your goal.

Daily Method of Operation (DMO)

Your Daily Method of Operation (DMO) is an intentional decision and plan of certain tasks you should be doing to promote growth or success in something that matters to you. The DMO includes the decision, plan, and action steps. Many of us have fallen into the "work every waking moment" trap with an efficient DMO because it was designed for our income producing activities. But, our Tribe can benefit from this strategy as well. We can reclaim our schedule making space for things that really give our life meaning. Creating a friendship DMO to build your Tribe is an excellent strategy that keeps this priority on your radar and advancing toward your goal.

Now that you have:

- made the decision to build and nurture your very own Tribe,
- daydreamed or brainstormed and journaled what your future Tribe looks like and how it makes you feel, and
- created a plan to meet new people, enhance current connections, and share more of yourself . . .

It's time to take action in an intentional, strategic way.

Step one can be accomplished by simply getting out your calendar and blocking out time for Tribe. It doesn't matter if you are old school pencil and paper, cutting edge calendar device savvy, or write-it-in-crayon on the family schedule that hangs on your fridge. It only matters that you document your strategy. If you don't have any kind of calendar system, get one!

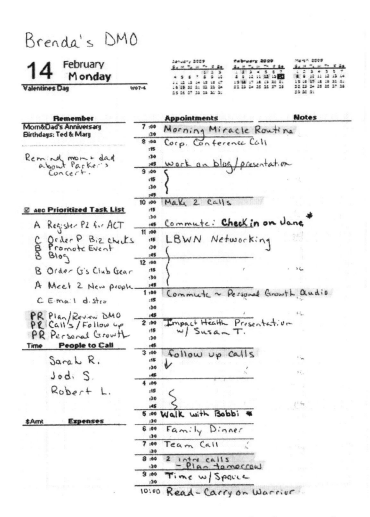

Step two is also simple, fun, and can be done simultaneously with step one. Take the initiative and reach out to some current friendships and schedule a date. This goes for current Tribe members and other women with whom you may want to go deeper. Together, find a time that works for both of you to get together one-on-one. The activity makes no difference—except that you have fun with it! This is not a *have too* appointment; it is a *get too* investment in your own well-being. If you have a friendship that you want to develop into Tribe, consider scheduling it weekly or every other week so you can accelerate building enthusiasm, history, and depth. Monthly is better than none, but this tactic will take longer. Remember, it takes about 40–60 hours of time spent together after meeting for people to form a casual friendship. To transition from a casual friend to a good friendship, you will need to be together for about 80–100 hours. From here to become close or best friends, it takes about 200 or more hours spent together. You get to decide how long it will take to reach Tribe status.

If you are just getting started or trying to find new members for your Tribe, step two will include scheduling activities where you will meet people. Join a running club that meets every Tuesday at the local brewery and connects over a beer after each run. Schedule in an art class Saturday mornings at "The Y" or recreation center. Sign up to volunteer once a month for a charity organization that has regular opportunities to help out.

You want to find recurring opportunities so that it is more likely you will see the same people a number of times. Use open body language to make yourself more approachable. In the beginning, what you do is just as important as what you say. Stand tall and squarely face the person you are speaking with. Maintain eye contact and gesture, nod or offer verbal affirmations occasionally to let them know you are listening. SMILE! It makes you more attractive and inviting to others.

Avoid crossing your arms, checking your phone, or standing off by yourself which implies that you are not open to connect.

Be the one who initiates conversation and follows up each time you see them with a warm greeting. Don't be interesting; be interested. Keep most of the attention on the person you are talking with. This demonstrates interest and selflessness in conversation. Being likeable is as easy as listening to people and asking them to tell you more. Everyone appreciates being seen and heard.

Take the initiative to get to know someone better. Set the next encounter in motion by proposing another meetup outside the current event. This will send a clear message that you are interested in being their friend.

Maybe you feel that meeting new people and being the inviter is scary. You may be apprehensive and your ego, that little bully voice in your head, tells you, "They probably won't like you. Don't go out on a limb. They will most likely reject you and your invitation." The more we think about it, the scarier it seems. This initial trepidation develops into a mental fear, which can take on a life of its own. This fear keeps us from making new friends.

Instead, assume people will like you! Hey! Let me remind you: you are awesome! Rather than fearing the worst, expect that most everyone in this group of strangers will love you and find you interesting. You can create your own self-fulfilling prophecy because we often get what we expect. If you go into social situations with a positive mindset, it is more likely that the outcome will be positive as well.

Although it may feel uncomfortable at first, know that your efforts to reach out will be appreciated. It is likely those new friends may feel the same way and are grateful to you for reaching out. While you are worried about the impression you are making, they are worried about the impression they are making. They are just as scared as you are. Share something about yourself and then ask them to share. Be the hero and save the connection! Have a playful attitude about it. This can be fun. If you decide to have a good time, or decide you won't, either way you will be right. Decisions are powerful.

Beyond planning dates and friend-finding activities, also schedule quick check-ins, thinking of you's, and phone calls. These drops in your friendship drip system are meaningful ways to build a Tribal foundation of support and validation. This sends a message that you are there for them, and they are on your mind, even when you aren't together. A check-in can be achieved by scheduling reminders on your smartphone to send a quick text, email an inspirational quote, or leave a voice message sharing a bit about your day. Plan a call to follow up on a conversation you had where a friend shared a concern with you. Ask her how it is going, encourage her, or offer help. Receiving a call like this is extremely validating and communicates that she has an ally in a tough situation. Adding this to your calendar may seem a bit calculated at first, and it is. We are establishing a good friendship habit. Soon it will become natural, and you will do it without thinking about it, let alone needing to schedule it.

Once you have done steps one and two, you have created your DMO. The final step three is simple and challenging at the same time. Step three is to protect those appointments at all costs! Guard them with your life!

It may seem harmless to allow urgent demands and requests to sideswipe your plans with Tribe. "Oh my friend will understand. . . . My boss asked me to work late, and I could use the extra cash. . . . My kids need a chaperone at the recreation center because the parent who set up the play date had something come up. . . . My husband needs me to pack for his business trip. . . .Can we reschedule?" As we begin to establish our new priority as it relates to Tribe, we must honor it with inflexibility! Lack of organization on the part of others should not constitute a contingency of your important friendship plan. As you begin to politely decline these urgent requests, you will be sending a message to those offenders that you value your Tribe-time—don't tread on me! Not to mention, if you allow them to run your life, you can expect those emergencies to continue to pop up. By guarding your Tribe-time, you are sending a clear message to your friend that she is a priority!

I recommend setting a time each week to plan and review step one and two of your DMO. It is helpful to review your calendar on a weekly basis to look ahead and strategize and schedule your priorities. Without a plan, your days and weeks may fly by at the whim of others' agendas. A solid DMO schedule will set you up for success by maximizing the time you can spend on the things you care about.

It is clear you care about friendship because you are reading this book. Remember a defining feature of friendship is that it is voluntary. It is not connected by wed, blood, or employment.

It is a relationship of great freedom and one that is retained only because we value it and intentionally give it our attention. Adult friendships don't happen organically, which is why we need to implement a strategy.

Carpe diem

Your DMO for Tribe has been thoughtfully and strategically designed. Now for the fun part. It is time for implementation. Seize the day! You will want to show up to your friendship dates with positive energy and enthusiasm.

A few hours before your meetup, do something that puts you in a good mood. Take a walk, listen to some energizing music, play with your kids or pets, give yourself a few minutes of quiet time. As you are traveling to see your friends, think about all the things about them you are grateful for.

The same method applies if you are going out to meet new people. Get yourself in a positive mood and then think about what strengths you are bringing to the new friendships that you seek. Are you funny, insightful, loyal, or reliable? Whatever your strengths may be, keep reminding yourself of them. As you walk into the event, tell yourself that people will like you and will be excited to meet you. This pre-paves the way in your mind and sets the stage for the outcome you desire.

The last tip I would like to suggest is consistency. As with any other worthwhile goal in life, friendship can benefit greatly from a persistent daily effort. I am reminded of a poster on the ceiling of the dentist I would visit as a child. You probably saw the same one. The message burned its image in my head as I was undergoing cavity removal. It said, "You don't have to floss all of your teeth, just the ones you want to keep." Like any other, good habits come from doing them daily. What one friendship habit can you do every day to benefit your Tribe? Maybe it is as simple as sending a daily text to one of your BFFs to let them know you care. Connect in some small way with one of them each and every day.

Trying something new and doing things differently can be challenging. It will require that you leave your current comfort zone for short periods of time. This may be awkward, especially as you get started. But, your dream is worth the effort. Your future Tribe is calling out to you and waiting for you to take these steps toward them with intention. What are you waiting for?

CHAPTER 12:

Strengthening Your Branches

ONCE YOU HAVE one or more friendships that you deem Tribeworthy, the quest is not over! As with almost any relationship, we must continue to invest in our Tribes. If they aren't growing, they may very well be decaying. Regular attention to our most valuable friendships is essential. Once you have resolved to accept no other outcome, all you need to do is create a routine, establish rituals, and do a little something every day for your Tribe.

Know your Tribe

How well do you really know your friends? Believe it or not, you may not know everything about even your lifelong friends! Maybe it is time to ask some questions. Make up your own friendship survey and send it to your gal-pals. You can include all kinds of fun questions to find out what makes them tick, lights their fire, and propels them to thrive. With this information you can do fun things to make them feel special. Remembering details that are meaningful to your Tribe members will surprise and delight them. When you create your survey, send it out with Google forms, and you will be able to make it into a spreadsheet if you are tech-savvy. Otherwise, send it by email—or even snail mail. We hardly get anything fun in the mail anymore. This will be a treat! Here are some examples of questions you can ask. Take what you like, add more, and make the questionnaire your own!

Sample Tribe Questionnaire

Please answer the following questions, and if there is a story behind one of your answers, please do share!

1. What is your favorite song & why?
2. When driving across the country, what are your go-to road trip snacks?
3. What is your favorite color?
4. Do you have a favorite holiday? Which one is it and why?
5. What is your favorite season? Why?
6. Do you have a hobby?

7. Is there something you have always wanted to try but haven't yet?

8. What is your favorite breakfast cereal?

9. How do you order your coffee?

10. What is your favorite:
    a. Wine
    b. Beer
    c. Cocktail

11. What is your favorite movie?

12. How do you relax?

13. What is your dream vacation?

14. What is your love language?

15. Do you have a favorite ice cream flavor?

16. What is your least favorite food?

17. If you had to pick one, would it be salty or sweet?

18. What is your favorite restaurant?

19. If you could eat one thing every day for the rest of your life and the calories didn't count, what would it be?

20. What is your favorite flower?

21. Do you have any phobias?

22. Pick one—facial or massage.

23. What is your favorite movie theater snack?

24. What is your favorite food or meal?

25. Your sweet tooth is acting up. What is it begging for?

Imagine how it would feel to receive this questionnaire. Knowing that someone cares enough about you to ask these questions would feel pretty good. Now let's go a bit deeper.

The next questions should be asked in person, over a cup of coffee or a glass of wine. Take turns answering each question. This will be an exercise in transparency and vulnerability that can uncover some ah-ha moments and strengthen your connection.

1. When we met, what was it about me that made you want to better know me?
2. What would you say are the three most important things that make our friendship work?
3. What trait do you most admire in me?
4. What is an immediate friendship turnoff?
5. We have busy lives. How can we best support each other?
6. How do you like to communicate and stay connected (text, phone, video chat, in person)?
7. If I ever felt that you were going down the wrong path, doing something that could possibly hurt you or be detrimental in any way, what would you like for me to do or say?
8. What is a trip, activity, or event that we can plan to do together? Something we can look forward to! (Tip: get the calendar out and start dreaming it up!)

These great questions will provide hours of entertainment and value, while at the same time increasing your understanding of each other. This exercise in and of itself moves the mark for both time and vulnerability quickly and in a significant way.

Discussions like these are intimate conversations that unite you closer to Tribe.

Monthly Moments

Ideally, we are able to connect with our Tribe members individually more than once a month. Our lives get busy with OPP (other people's priorities) as well as work, family fun, and commitments. It is easy to let weeks or even months slip by if we are not intentional about our own priorities.

Earlier we discussed adopting a DMO system to plan our weeks and months. This method will keep your priorities in the forefront and documented. An appointment that is scheduled on your calendar is easier to defend from the OPP than a loose plan floating around in your head! Here are some ideas for types of monthly gatherings and activities to add to your calendar.

Schedule a Monthly Girls Night Out

Girls Night Out, we call it GNO, can be anything that interests your group of friends. Maybe it is dinner, drinks, and dancing. Perhaps it is signing up for an art class like Paint & Sip, pottery making, or painting. How about a monthly cooking class where you can all learn some new culinary skills while sipping wine and then enjoying the product together at the end? This group of friends can include your Kindred Clan aka—Tribe exponential!

Each month you could get dressed up and together treat yourself to a fancy restaurant and share a bougier-than-usual bottle of wine and some Parmesan garlic fries for the table. Another idea is to grab some cheap tickets to a local sporting event. Your Tribe can kick it in the nosebleed section with nachos and beer. Find out what the future has in store for you by sharing a visit to a psychic. Together you can dissect the experience over lunch. How about Glow in the Dark Bowling? Wear your best 70s attire, as there is often a retro glow about the evening. Let out your inner roller girl at a local rink. Yes, they still exist and even have adult nights. Coordinate your Tribe's dress code and take the venue by storm. These are just a few ideas. For new ideas each month, join Lady and the Tribe's Vision Quest newsletter at www.LadyAndTheTribe.com.

My ladies gather monthly for Women Who Wine. Here is how it works: each year we have 12 volunteer hostesses who sign up to welcome our Clan into her home. At the beginning of the month, an Evite is sent out to our Tribe, Kindred Clan, and new friendships saved in a contact group. It includes the details: hostess and address, date, start time and end time. It includes an end time because our event is on a school/work night. We have such a great time, and the time passes so quickly, we could stay too long and regret it the next day! Many guests are able to stop by for a bit because it doesn't take the whole evening, and the end time gives guests an easy time to politely slip out. The end time also protects the hostess from guests staying too long, yet allows them to extend the event if they choose. The hostess provides only the starters which include a bottle of wine, and an appetizer. Each guest is asked to *bring their own wine glass* and contribute one item.

1. A bottle of wine (or)
2. An appetizer (or)
3. Something sweet

This plan provides structure to ensure there is plenty of everything and that the workload is dispersed. The hostess is not overwhelmed by cooking all day, nor does she have the expense of feeding a dozen or more hungry ladies! The hostess also does not need to have dozens of wine glasses available, and the dirty dishes just return home with the guests. Our monthly gathering has been going on for years, and we have it down like clockwork.

I highly recommend scheduling one ongoing monthly event for your girlfriends. It's something you can always count on. In the event that you can't always attend, the tradition carries on in your absence, yet you can be sure you will be missed. This monthly event will become one of the pillars of your Tribe's connectivity.

Schedule 1:1 Tribe-Time

Make a goal to see your Tribe no less than a few times each month, connecting between visits with phone calls, texts, and video chats. The monthly GNO event certainly counts, but it is a great idea to get each of your Tribemates on your calendar individually as well. These 1:1 meetups are great for personal conversations, updates, and helping each other work through private issues. A friendly ear, some good advice, and a person with whom we can share our concerns is often a welcome release. This is a chance to be there for each other through the trials, tribulations, and triumphs in our lives. We are in this together; we are Tribe.

Girl's Weekend Trips

Raise your hand if you have ever said to a girlfriend, "We should totally plan a girl's trip to _____!" Have you done it yet? What is stopping you? Our minds will always give us a hundred reasons why we can't do something if that is what we are looking for. The 2019 AAA Girlfriend Travel Research Project says that 24% of women have taken a girlfriend getaway in the past three years.[72] Ladies and Tribes, I think we can do better!

Something special happens when you physically gather women, escape your everyday lives, and vacation with your girlfriends. The following are some of the many benefits you may experience.

1. You are removed from the everyday noise and distractions of your life.
2. You are cared for, nourished, and surrounded by mother-like love.
3. You enter a place of spiritual refreshing and renewing.
4. You may help prepare a meal, but you will also be served a meal or more.
5. You disconnect from the day-to-day drudgery, if only for a few nights.
6. You share experiences with your girlfriends and deepen your relationships.

7. You have concentrated time together with your Tribe.
8. You will experience "Ah-ha—*I see your soul!*" moments and will also be seen.
9. You will enjoy female adult conversations.
10. You will laugh; you will cry; and your heart will overflow with validation.
11. You will return home filled with appreciation and a newfound sense of serenity. You will be ready to take on your own world again

As women, our shared feminine energy is magnetic, and we are naturally drawn to each other. We empathize with our similarities, and our sixth sense of intuition helps us understand each other. The united energy that is created at a girl's retreat becomes a powerful healing force bonding us at a higher level.

Your retreat can be less than an hour's drive or across the globe. It's all up to you! I recommend one annual retreat that is within driving distance, somewhere between one hour and three, so your scenery changes in a significant way. Plan it out six to nine months in advance, so you all have something to look forward to. Preparing and getting excited for the retreat is all part of the fun and is bonding in and of itself.

Our annual GNO Retreat is always in the mountains. Our real-world escape is three nights, although some are only able to get away for two—and that is okay! The first-day ladies head out as soon as they can; some arrive early to catch a hike on the front end. Others leave in time to meet up for a late lunch before check-in. The rest head up as soon as they are off work.

We rent a big house . . . a mansion of sorts that has a real bed for every one of us. We have had as many as sixteen attend! When we split the price of a huge manor by ten or more, we manage to keep the price affordable for all. We find something with a gourmet kitchen, a hot tub, a fire pit, and comfy spaces to gather. That first evening, we all bring an appetizer to share, and of course, oodles of cocktails enter the equation as soon as we are settled. Once we are gathered for the evening, we facilitate an intention-setting icebreaker of some sort usually led by our Tribe's soul seraph.

Day two, ladies wake to the scrumptious scent of breakfast being prepared by one of the meal teams. The beauty of the weekend is that you get to be served and eat all weekend and only need to help purchase, plan, and prepare one of the four main meals. We enjoy breakfast together. Ladies are in and out of the hot tub and then off in mini-groups to go shopping, hiking, or to hit the spa. Some take advantage of a little quiet time and stay back to enjoy the property. We re-assemble at a designated time for another fabulous meal, vino, and a connecting activity. Day three is similar to day two, however, we often throw in a chick flick that evening for some while others solve the problems of the world around the kitchen table.

The next morning, we are always shocked at how the weekend flew by. Everyone heads down the mountain at various times, but before we leave one another, we share one last Tribe ritual that usually involves gratitude and recognition of what each member brought to the weekend. Every member leaves feeling as if they have been deeply seen, heard, and known in a more meaningful way than ever before.

Your mission, should you choose to accept it, is to poll your closest friends and nail down a date when everyone can escape for a weekend. This may need to be scheduled out months from now, but that is perfect! You will have enough time to guard and protect that date as well as enjoy the planning process. Girl's weekend date will get here before you know it!

Girl's Weekend on a Budget

You CAN get away with your girlfriends on any budget. Renting a mansion is not a requirement, but I highly recommend it! For food, fuel, and mansion expenses, our group spends less than $300 per person for four days, three nights. If need be, it could be done for much less.

Planning your expedition months in advance will allow you to put a little away each week or month. There are nice home rentals on VRBO or Airbnb that you can acquire at very reasonable prices and can fit almost any budget. You can cut expenses by bringing most of your own food and beverages. Going out all the time is fun but can get pricey. Cooking together is also fun and can add more experiences to your Tribe's history book.

Look into the FREE activities in the area that you will be visiting. There may be community festivals and local events already happening that you can tap into. Maybe there is a farmer's market, a local historic attraction, or an art exhibit that you can roam.

Here's another idea: create your own workshop! Have a mastermind session on a topic or book of interest. Pick up some wine glasses from a thrift shop and some acrylic paints and brushes. You can host your own creativity session, and as a bonus . . . you have a built-in souvenir to take home!

Can't afford Macy's and the mall? Scout out nearby thrift, pawn, and consignment shops, and go treasure hunting! Once upon a time I would have said, "That is not for me!" However, my sister opened my eyes to the adventure of bargain shopping, and since then, I have found so many unique and prized items.

How about creating your own *Top Chef* or baking contest? Contestants can compete for the title, GNO Cuisine Queen, and the judges can have fun heckling the contestants: "Please pack your knives and GO" or "Get the Fudge Out!" Everyone can enjoy the winning creations as well as those of the runner's up!

Channel your inner supermodel. Before dinner one night, ask everyone to pull out their bold makeup, big hair, and clubbing attire. Get dolled up! Even though you are eating in, you can still dress to the nines. "I'm too Sexy for your party, too sexy for your party. No way I'm disco dancing" . . . well maybe. Have a mini photo shoot to find your next profile pic. Strike a pose—VOGUE. It will make for a great time and some fabulous Instagram posts.

Can you say karaoke? No need for all the equipment of yesteryear! If you have a FREE YouTube account, you are set. Add a smart TV . . . you are golden! You will find almost any song's karaoke version is available at your fingertips. Pull everyone up to participate. They may not admit it, but everyone loves to sing.

For new ideas each month, join Lady and the Tribe's Vision Quest newsletter at www.LadyAndTheTribe.com. Here are 20 more ways to enjoy girls' weekend spending little or no money:

- Pamper party manicures and pedicures
- Hike the local trails
- Game night!
- Movies and popcorn
- Have a fondue party
- Be a tourist; see the sights
- Plan a high tea
- Host an *Amazing Race* team building activity
- Play tennis, pickle ball, or lawn games
- Bring scrapbooks or other crafts
- Tour a local museum or art show
- Create Dream Boards together
- Practice yoga
- Binge watch the Hallmark Channel
- Be lazy and relax—you have permission
- Learn something new
- Volunteer as a group
- Go for a bike ride together
- Star gaze, sit on the porch, and share a dream
- Mentor and support a friend in need

The Amazing Women

Meet Krista, Pam, Michelle, Suzy, and Jana. They are a remarkable Tribe of women who have been traveling together three to four times every year for almost a decade. A few of them met through work, and the rest became acquainted in a travel-related business. They all LOVE to travel, had some fun times with this venture, and decided they wanted to spin off the idea and create their own "cheap" getaways. They hardly even knew each other when they embarked on their first weekend getaway, yet the bonds they have created with intention have been life changing.

They call their group the "Amazing Women," and they have some unique "rules" for their signature adventures. First and most importantly, the budget is $150 per person. Once you commit to going, you must pay whether you go or not. One Tribe member makes all the plans and handles the money. Most of the time this is a "mystery trip." The rest of the Tribe does not know where they are going until travel day. The planner gives a trip packing list and maybe a clue or two. The $150 must cover everything but the booze—you're on your own for that! Included are all travel expenses: transportation, food, and activities.

They decided to make this an inexpensive quarterly event, so they could see each other more often and not just have one big annual trip that quickly comes and goes. Also, since they are spending so little, they don't feel as bad using family funds and leaving the fam behind. Some members feel guilty spending money on themselves, but the $150 isn't so bad.

Oh, the interesting and memorable times the Amazing Women have shared! They have done things they never would have considered if not for the challenge of entertaining themselves on a low-to-no budget. Tour a Chicken Coop in Galveston? It was FREE! They had to do it! Visit an Eclectic Art Show? Absolutely! Suzy was the first to get them all on a plane within the budget. Upon discovering this revelation, Krista exclaimed with glee, "Suzy is getting us on a plane! I can't believe it!" One weekend they visited BOTH New York City and Chicago—WOW!

"We are all moms," Michelle explains. "We are always planning everything. It is so nice to just show up, have it all planned, and be told what to do." Jana admits being a self-proclaimed type "A" control freak. "Now it is okay, but it was really hard at first. One time, we were told we could only bring one backpack and pack only what we could fit in a shoebox . . . really? Yep!" Another time they were told not to bring any food!

Pam rebelled but then had to relinquish her popcorn to the car rental guy. However, they scored a free automobile upgrade in the process! If there's a deal to be found, Pam will find it.

When asked, "What does Tribe-time do for you?" Pam shares, "Knowing that these women are part of my life and always there for me gives me peace of mind." Michelle explains that she feels re-energized by the Tribe. Known as the "serious one" of the bunch, she loosens up and even gets a little silly. Krista finds an overall sense of play and connection. She says, "We share some seriously deep stuff like God, marriage, and work . . . but also just do silly stupid stuff. I can drink if I want, smoke if I want, take a nap if I want, not shower if I want. I can do whatever I want. As women, we don't remember how to play because we are the caretakers, doers, and givers in our everyday lives. On girls' trips, that all goes out the window, and our playfulness comes back to us. We are wearing wigs, going dancing, watching movies, listening to music, and eating junk food."

Jana shares that when she met this group, she was a young mother with three little ones, and she had never "left" for a weekend away from the family, which had been more than seven years. "So this was my first experience just being 'me' again after becoming a mom. I felt like I could re-center to who I was outside of that role.

It brings me back to who I am." Suzy was just recently divorced when she joined the Tribe. She immediately felt comfortable, like she was in a no-judgment zone. "It feels like I can be me with these women."

The Amazing Women have encouragement for other women who aren't "here" yet. Suzy recalls sharing the advice she gave her 26-year-old daughter. "Friendship doesn't just happen. You need to build it, get a little vulnerable, and go out on a limb. If you do this and she is your person, you will know it, and you may have made a friend for life." Jana suggests "Just take the first step and remember you must nurture relationships. What you give up by taking that risk you will get back tenfold. It makes me a better wife and mother."

Krista explains, "You may not have a friend that you have been on trips with for ten years or a group to travel with… YET. It just starts with a conversation. It starts with a book club, a church group, or a meetup. If you meet a woman who is interesting, invite her over for dinner and see what happens. You never have to see her again if you don't want to. You may not find a BFF, but you will always get something out of it. If you have a hard time putting yourself out there, learn to ask a lot of questions; everyone loves to talk about themselves. You get to learn a lot about people, and you are also interviewing them to see if you want to hang out with them more. You never know when a simple conversation is going to turn into a lifelong friendship.

Jana shared a story about a friend of hers who "wanted a group." Her friend explained, "I know a lot of people, but I don't have a lot of close friends". She decided to invite every woman she knew, like sixty ladies, to a party. Jana said her impression was that this friend was super popular. She was very involved in the community. "I thought she had dozens of close friends. I had no idea she didn't feel like she had any close friends." We have all felt at times not necessarily excluded but not included. Reach out because someone else is probably feeling the exact same way. Jana's friend's party was a success! She is still searching and building her Tribe but she did collect a few new friendships.

Over the years the Amazing Women's trips have brought them incredibly close and provided many interesting stories. Yes, the budget is still only $150. At one point, the event started taking on a life of its own, challenging the organizer to go bigger and better each time. However, they soon realized that it just didn't matter where they went. As long as they were together as Tribe, they would have a ball.

The Daily Grind and Special Occasions

It may seem odd to have daily grind and special occasions grouped together. Nevertheless, any day can become a special occasion! The daily and weekly routine we establish with a DMO can facilitate meaningful moments all throughout the year.

Special occasions like birthdays and holidays are obvious opportunities to let our Tribe know they are important to us. Tribes also benefit by creating their own celebratory traditions. In case you didn't know, as I did not until writing this book, National Girlfriends Day is August 1! Lady and the Tribe will certainly be celebrating that going forward.

Knowing our best friends well will help us see other opportunities to take notice and make their day. A new job, promotion, closing a big sale, completing a big test, winning a tennis match, and finishing a project all can be reasons to celebrate your Tribe's wins. Recognition, cheering, and applause—enough to make a girl blush—is highly encouraged. Something as simple as a handwritten note of encouragement or appreciation can make a day special to the recipient. Every day we are blessed with in this lifetime is worth celebrating. We only need to remember and remind our Tribe to do so.

Sharing Your Story

As I began the project of collecting data and research for Lady and the Tribe, I asked my friends to share their friendship stories. I wanted to hear about friendship moments that were meaningful to them in their own words. I also wanted their help recalling our own escapades, so I could be a better storyteller. Having received several of these friendship stories, I realized that the product I have received from each of them is a cherished gift. Although each story was written very differently, I found myself laughing and crying tears of joy as I recalled these precious moments. I highly encourage you to write down and share some of your friendship stories. I was so touched by my friend Lauri's friendship story I chose to share it in its entirety.

Lauri

I believe that I have the best friends ever—friends that I have had since high school and then reconnected with when we all ended back up in Colorado. I moved to Iowa after high school and moved back in 1995. My friend, Brenda, had just helped me find a new job, and my first day landed on Valentine's Day. So, I was in the office for around two hours when I was called to the front desk to pick up a beautiful bouquet of flowers waiting for me from my "secret admirer." I had no clue who they could be from, however, it was a great icebreaker, and I met a lot of my coworkers due to it being my first day and already getting flowers. Best first day ever! When I got home, I asked Brenda if she had sent the flowers, and she denied it. A few months later, I got a card in the mail with a bunch of my friends' signatures. They were the ones who sent the flowers. Brenda had organized the whole thing to make my first day memorable.

One of my biggest blessings are the Ridgley's and the fact that they have entrusted me with their children. My happiest times have been when I was able to give back to Brenda and Parker for always supporting me by watching their kids, whether they were on a cruise or just a long weekend getaway. Those kids have my heart as do their parents.

I have great friends from various stages in my life. A good friend that I made at another company, Donna, supported me during one of my most difficult times. My mother called me late one night to tell me my dad had passed. My parents lived in Longmont, Colorado, and I lived in Parker, Colorado—an hour's drive. Needless to say, I was in no shape to make that drive. I called Donna at 11:00 p.m., and she immediately offered to drive me to my parent's house. She stayed with me and helped my family the whole week and held my hand during the rosary and the funeral. She had to take vacation time to be there, but she never hesitated. Her support was amazing, and I'll forever be grateful for her.

Another one of my favorite friendship stories was my 40th birthday. I had filed for divorce and was in a huge transitional phase in my life. I was getting healthy, mentally, emotionally, and physically. By reconnecting with friends I had drifted away from during my marriage, I was finding myself again. Brenda, always there for me, coordinated with a bunch of my girlfriends to celebrate my birthday week. Yes, week! Different friends had different days. I was taken to lunch. I got a pedicure, massage, haircut and highlights, a makeover and all new makeup, new outfits— basically, a week of pampering. It was amazing!! My heart was full. Nothing could top the week I had. That Saturday, Brenda arranged for us to go to dinner to finish celebrating my birthday with a group of our friends. They even rented a limo. I was not paying any attention to where we're going, and we needed to stop by and pick up our friend, Dani. When we pulled up to the house, they told me to go grab Dani. I got out of the limo, saw a line of parked cars, and realized they had arranged for a surprise party for me! So many great friends from high school and my job, friends that I had made through my ex-husband, my family, and kids from my neighborhood. They had a box they gave me with notecards that everyone had written on . . . what they loved about me. It was truly the best day I have ever had. I still have that box, and when I'm feeling down, I can read those cards and remember that I am loved and valued. (I get weepy anytime I talk about that day—that week.) I am blessed.

Brenda, I'm sure I could come up with more stories. So many of them with you in them. I know you said they don't need to be about only our friendship, but truly most of my best friendship stories involve you. You've always been such a huge cheerleader for me. You encourage me, push me outside my comfort zone (i.e., signing me up that first year for the Las Vegas Marathon relay team or making me "fill in" for softball), support me, love me, and include me. I can't imagine what my life would have been without you. I want to be the first to purchase your book and have you sign it for me. Then I want to buy copies for all my girlfriends. I hope you know that I love you and respect you. I believe in you and support you in anything you choose to do. I have never doubted that you could do anything you've set out to do. You INSPIRE me. I love you so much and I'm so blessed to be part of your Tribe and your family.

~ Lauri

As I read her words again, I'm holding back tears. At the time, I did not think any of the gestures she described were a big deal. I do love making Lauri feel special. She is the kind of friend that you like to incessantly tease because she is such a fun, easygoing target. She is probably the most loyal person I know.

We met when we were 17 working at McDonalds. You may laugh, but it was a great place to work. We learned how to do a wide variety of jobs, each of which had a system in place. It was hard work, but the organization made it fun with opportunities for competition. It was fast-paced and busy! So many people came through the doors—high school friends, family, and so many others. I think I had worked there almost a year when Lauri started working with me, and before too long, we were fast friends.

Lauri is also a connector. Even in high school, she was the one to call everyone to make our weekend and summer plans. It was great. I think I often made the plan, and Lauri would communicate it. All I did after that was show up and have a blast. We had our own little Tribe at the time that we called our crew.

Lauri was due to return to a rival high school in the fall, the beginning of our senior year. Surprisingly, we convinced her to transfer . . . her senior year . . . to attend our high school. To this day, Lauri continues to connect us, consistently show up in surprising ways, and support our crazy adventures.

She stood with me as a bridesmaid on my wedding day. She is my son's First Communion sponsor and my daughter's Godmother. Lauri is truly a magnanimous friend, Tribe for a lifetime, and the family I choose.

The Little Things Mean A Lot

There is no need for grand gestures of friendship in Tribe. It is the little things we do everyday, every week, every month, and every year that add up and create our friendship stories. The point is to be mindful of your priorities, and if building your own Tribe is important, you will find a way to make it happen. Systemizing your schedule may sound pragmatic in friendship, but it is effective. As with any goal, keep it in front of you with a plan, protect your Tribe-time, and do a little something every day. We strengthen our tree of life branches with the basics—regular attention, appreciation, and nourishment.

CHAPTER 13:

Quest for Wholeness

WE ALL WANT to be whole. At some point in time, we may find ourselves asking the universe, "What is the meaning of life? What is my purpose? Why do I feel like something is missing?" I found myself asking these questions the year my son was a senior in high school and began planning for college. He had decided to go to a performing arts school in New York, far away from our home in Colorado. I was experiencing some inner turmoil as I realized my life, as I had come to know it, was about to undergo an unwelcome transformation.

As many mothers do, I had spent the last 18 years focusing on my family and much of my identity revolved around that role. What purpose did I have beyond raising good kids? Oh, how I would miss my son . . . and then I would soon be losing my daughter too. Things were never going to be the same again. Our family of four, my world, was a ticking time bomb soon to implode. I struggled to hang on to every possible MOM-ent that school year.

I felt an unexplainable emptiness creep up on me. My life was great, but something was missing. I wasn't motivated to do anything beyond clinging to the upcoming "lasts" of a child becoming a young man. I longed for a new goal, purpose, or intention to get excited about, but I was not finding the inspiration. In an attempt to find my way, I wrote this letter to the universe.

Dear Universe,

I have heard the analogy that our energy stream is like a river; we should work with the current, rather than paddle upstream. We can be or do or have anything we want, believe, and allow. Everything we want is downstream. All we need to do is turn our boat around and paddle with the current, our inspired action, or let the oars go altogether and let the momentum take us to our best life. I sometimes feel like I turned the boat around and drifted into a large lake with little current, or my boat was dropped in the middle of the ocean, and I'm lost at sea. The only way out is to paddle. But, I don't feel the inspirational current, and

I don't see the destination clearly. My question to the Universe is: "How long do I hang out in this boat adrift being content but not satisfied?" I love the peace I have found, but I am hungry for inspiration and passion to drive me into motivated action. "When will I hit the rapids again and find the current that makes the journey seem effortless and exciting?" I feel incomplete without a burning desire. There it is, Universe. "What do I do next?" I am so grateful for all of the blessings in my life. I have many. Life is beautiful. I want back in the game of contribution and creation . . . eagerness and excitement . . . joyfully making a difference. "Isn't it okay to want it all?"

All my love,
Brenda

My letter was not immediately answered. It took some time, but months later, I did find my way out of this funk. In the early spring as we approached graduation day, I was dreading the last-last, thinking about all the things I would soon be missing and having a little pity party for myself. Out of the blue I received an ah-ha moment—a message from my inner being. My mind flipped the switch, and instead of dwelling on the things I would miss, I began to get excited about what I would "get to do" when I became an empty nester.

I would get to spend more time with my girlfriends! My calendar wouldn't be overcrowded with family commitments, sports calendars, and fundraisers. I could hike more with Bobbi and Michelle! Parker and I would be free to travel anywhere and on a moment's notice! Jane and I could brainstorm new entrepreneurial adventures! I could redecorate the house, enhance the patio, and declutter! I could go shopping and have lunch with Jenny and Lauri more often! I could do something completely different and new! I could recreate myself for this new chapter. Who do I want to be?

I realized the inner turmoil I had allowed stemmed from what I anticipated as a loss of connection. The hands-on part of my motherhood journey was coming to an end. The upcoming lack of proximity to my son and daughter created a hole in my spirit that Facetime and text messages were not going to fill. My kids would soon be finding, building, and nurturing new relationships to create the next chapter in their lives, and I needed to do the same thing.

Blessed with a great man in my life and a strong marriage, I began to focus more on our couplehood as man and wife rather than our roles that dominated the past decades as father and mother. I turned to my best friends with new vigor and set the intention to nurture those connections to an even deeper level. I came to realize how blessed I was to have this handful of loving, supportive, and true women in my life.

This book is written in their honor and also for every woman who has sometimes given just a little too much and lost herself along the way. Throughout this book, we have discussed our need to connect, our need to be part of something, and our longing to belong and be known. We need our Tribe to make us healthy and whole. Lifelong friendships who will root for us celebrate our victories and hold us when things fall apart.

One Tribe at a time, we can change the world by reconnecting to what gives our life meaning and brings us joy. Just imagine a society composed of individuals who all felt loved, supported, and known by not one, but a handful of impenetrable relationships. Friendships bound by choice, not birthright, marriage, or contract—a comrade for every occasion possessing a vast breadth of knowledge, skills, gifts, and abilities. A sisterhood of connections extending further than our BFFs, through circles of Kindred Clan and beyond, exemplifying the fact that we are ALL connected.

If we all felt connected, wouldn't we treat the stranger on the street with more care? Would we not welcome the newcomer with more enthusiasm? Would we not seek to understand our differences before jumping to conclusions? Competition and contests could be reserved for fun and expansion as intended. Debate could be a tool for decision-making and clarification rather than making others look foolish. Would it not be easier to love one another?

I challenge you to become the leader of your own Tribe today and join our Lady and the Tribe Inner Circle at www. LadyAndTheTribe.com. To find, nurture, and build a Tribe, all it takes is a decision, a plan, and action. Keep your efforts growing with your attention, persistence, and a little TLC.

We are one. Our suffering happens when we forget that. We can fill up that hollow spot in our spirits with the fullness only meaningful connections can occupy. No matter where we are on our Tribal Quest, we now have the knowledge and tools to find new friendships, nurture the ones we have, and create a network of support that will last a lifetime. When three or more of us gather together, we are a Tribe.

APPENDIX:
THE DATA

AS I EMBARKED on writing *Lady and the Tribe,* I began to research dozens of friendship books and close to 100 articles and blogs. I decided to conduct my own independent research as well and compiled data collected from 153 respondents in the Find Your Tribe Friendship Questionnaire. The questionnaire was predominantly marketed through Facebook and Instagram on social media. The questions and data collected were not designed to achieve scientific result status but rather to provide a significant sample of responses on components correlated with Tribe.

The respondents identified themselves as 88.9% female and 10.5% male with .6% preferring not to say. Of the respondents, 47.7% identified themselves in the 50–59 age group, and 43.4% were between the ages of 30 and 49 and 60 to 69 represented 9.8%. I was pleased with these statistics, as I intended to write *Lady and the Tribe* for women who have experienced some life changes and could perhaps benefit the most from this information.

The questions that followed were designed to get an idea of where this population of "social media" savvy individuals landed on topics of friendship. The fact that they participate on social media tells me that they value social connection. One could also assume that the statistics collected may not accurately represent the grander population that includes those who do not actively engage on social media.

You may notice that a number of the questions are similar. This is strategic. The questions are asked that way to get the respondents to really consider their close connections. As I share the results, I ask you to consider your answer to each question and see where you fall as compared to this social media connected sample group.

The Results

1. How often do you see your very closest friends?
    *   Daily - 4.7%
    *   Weekly - 23.8%
    *   Monthly - 51%
    *   Yearly - 20.5%

These results are encouraging, as a large part of this group has habits of connecting in person. Those with daily and weekly habits are likely to consider these friendships BFFs or Tribe. Monthly attention to a friendship resembles maintenance mode. You don't lose ground, but you aren't building intimacy. Of this group 20% has not established regular Tribe or Kindred Clan time but connects with her soul sisters/brothers on occasion.

2. How many friends do you have in your life right now who you can count on to help you when you need it?
   - 0 - 1.2%
   - 1 - 3.3%
   - 2 - 7.9%
   - 3 - 12.4%
   - 4 - 15.7%
   - 5+ - 59.5%

In hindsight, this question was too vague. The answer I was trying to achieve would have been better asked, "How many friends do you have who you could you call in the middle of the night if you had car trouble?" The point of the question goes beyond *helping you out* but rather having a close enough friend you would be comfortable asking them to go out of their way to the point of discomfort. That being said, still 12% had two or fewer people to call and there were some zeros reported. Everyone needs a few of these ICE (In Case of Emergency) friendships.

3. How many friends do you trust with private/personal information?
   - 0 - 6.3%
   - 1 - 8.2%
   - 2 - 19.7%
   - 3 - 15.8%
   - 4 - 16.4%
   - 5+ - 33.6%

   This question taps into one's vulnerability. These numbers share that most of the respondents are practicing transparency with their friendships. Everyone needs someone to confide in outside of family. A handful is nice but at least 2–3 would be ideal.

4. How many of your friends do you feel really *know* you? They know the good, bad, and ugly and love you anyway.
   - 0 - 5.2%
   - 1 - 12.4%
   - 2 - 19%
   - 3 - 18.3%
   - 4 - 13.7%
   - 5+ - 31.4%

5. How many people can you trust enough to tell secrets too?
   - 0 - 7.2%

- 1 - 11.1%
- 2 - 24.8%
- 3 - 17%
- 4 - 9.8%
- 5+ - 30.1%

It is important to have a confidante, someone you can share a secret with. Sharing a personal secret can help you gain perspective on a situation that is concerning you. This need-to-know status of information would usually have a very limited number of shares. You may have different confidantes depending on the dilemma or information.

6. How many people would have your back when others criticize you?
   - 0 - 2.9%
   - 1 - 4.3%
   - 2 - 11.1%
   - 3 - 14.4%
   - 4 - 13.7%
   - 5+ - 53.6%

Over half of the respondents feel secure in that they have five or more people who would defend their honor. That is a good feeling and a good reason to intentionally build these strong friendships. *Your people* are on *your team* in the event of controversy.

7. How many people make you feel special, appreciated, and loved?
   - 0 - 3.5%
   - 1 - 5.1%
   - 2 - 11.8%
   - 3 - 10.5%
   - 4 - 9.9%
   - 5+ - 59.2%

Validation is the name of the game when it comes to feeling appreciated. It authenticates who you are and how your contributions are valued. Every soul on this earth deserves to feel loved. When it comes to authentic appreciation, the more the merrier. It is a significant benefit of Tribe.

8. How many friends do you have who believe in you? They encourage you to "go for it" even when it appears to be a BIG challenge.
   - 0 - 3.9%
   - 1 - 4%
   - 2 - 15%
   - 3 - 15.7%
   - 4 - 9.8%
   - 5+ - 51.6%

When someone believes in you, everything can change. Our fears decrease, and our confidence increases, making us courageous enough to aim higher. These friendships illuminate our best qualities. When someone is specific about why they believe in you, it can often make you more aware of and more confident in your strengths. They teach us to believe in ourselves. When someone truly believes in you, the feeling becomes contagious. When someone boasts about your best qualities, focusing on your strengths rather than your limitations, it changes the way you think and feel about yourself. Our Tribe becomes our cheerleaders and propels us forward toward our dreams.

9. How many friends do you have who will call you out when you are getting off track and/or hold you accountable? These friends are completely honest with you, even when the truth hurts.
   - 0 - 5.1%
   - 1 - 17.8%
   - 2 - 27.6%
   - 3 - 17.1%
   - 4 - 11.2%
   - 5+ - 21.1%

Here we see a significant shift in the percentage of friends who will deliver unpopular news or even criticism. These frank friendships are important, and like family, they care enough about you to have the hard conversations. As we are looking for these

Tribe friendships, we want to model the behavior we are looking for, so here are some tips on delivering disapproval:

- Leave the brutal part out of the honest discussion. It is important to be direct yet respectful when offering constructive criticism.
a. Set the stage sharing how much you care about them. Explain that you are bringing up this issue because you are concerned.
b. Be curious about the situation, keeping the conversation open and considerate. It is also important to be clear and concise.
c. If it comes down to a difference of opinion, make your point and leave it, so they can think about it. No one wants to hear someone go on and on.

It is nice to think that our friends are always going to support us and be on board with our shenanigans. Realistically, we will have some disagreements with our closest friendships, and Tribe is no exception. We truly want this feedback, as it comes from a place of love, and sometimes we need someone else's perspective to stay on track.

10. How many friends do you have on social media?
- None (I don't do social media) - 0.9%
- 1-100 - 12.4%

- 101-500 - 43.8%
- 501-1000 - 19.6%
- 1000+ - 20.3%
- 5000+ (I have reached my friends limit) - 3%

After watching the Netflix documentary, *The Social Dilemma*, I discovered that, along with many other Americans and humans worldwide, I am addicted to social media. This docudrama suggests that social media is designed to nurture an addiction, manipulate people and governments, and spread conspiracy theories and disinformation. The documentary also examines its effects on mental health. If it's all true, the issues the film raises are deeply concerning. Regardless, it made me question my own social media habits and intentionally make changes.

The film noted habits like the compulsion to check your phone for social media updates, even when you haven't heard a notification. Another is the fear of being out of WIFI range (nomophobia) . . . really . . . it's an issue. The worst thing is being on your device while you are spending time with friends and family. Are we more interested in witnessing other's selectively shared lives than living our own? It would appear so. However, it's more likely a bad habit. An addiction we must acknowledge and address.

I am not here to say you should stop using social media. I intend to continue using it as a way to stay connected and as a tool to share positivity and helpful information. I do suggest that we each take our own inventory of how we are using social media: how often, for how long, and how it makes us feel.

As it relates to Tribe, social media can be a tool in your friendship drip system. Sharing fun memories, tagging your friends, and commenting on things that bring you joy are great ways to connect on a surface level. There are many business applications to social media as well. This is both good and bad. As you are seeking social connection, just keep in mind you are being marketed to at the same time. Social media can help you stay connected to your soul sisters, Kindred Clan, and community. However, it will not deepen your relationships to a significant extent.

11. Based on the previous answers, how many friends are in your Tribe? (Tribe = the very closest of friends)
    - 0 - 3.6%
    - 1 - 5.2%
    - 2 - 11.8%
    - 3 - 16.4%
    - 4 - 22.4%
    - 5+ - 40.8%

This group of respondents self-scored their Tribe status pretty high, and perhaps they are spot on. As a group, they shared that they generally have strong socializing habits both with and without technology. However, their reported numbers in the questions involving vulnerability did not score quite as high as this reflects. If you consider that Tribe = Friendship + Space + Vulnerability, Tribe members should be strong in each of these areas.

I also believe some, although instructed otherwise, included their spouse in their Tribe. Obviously, one's spouse is a significant person in your social life and perhaps your #1 ally. Several respondents commented that their spouse was their best friend. That is truly lovely, however, not the same relationship we are seeking as in a Tribe of friendships. The dynamics are completely different when we are not bound by law, finances, and intimate relations. Our Tribe is that extra layer of support, disconnected just enough to offer a valuable perspective and unconditional love.

12. Does your significant other support and encourage the friendships you have in your Tribe?
    - Never - .8
    - Sometimes - 9.2%
    - Frequently - 9.2%
    - Always - 56.2%

- N/A - 24.8%

I was just curious about this, and I am glad to see the majority have a spouse who, like I do, encourages their friendships. Female friendships are good for us and, in effect, good for our spouse because we are more likely to be happy and content in our lives. In kind, we should also support our spouse's friendships for the same reason. Couple friends are nice, but each partner will benefit from having their own friends independently. Our marriages can be stronger when we are whole, and our friendships help make us so.

13. Do you have someone you consider to be your best friend?
    - Yes - 80.9%
    - No - 19.1%

In addition to the multiple-choice questions, the Find Your Tribe Friendship Questionnaire had another eight questions that respondents could answer directly in their own words. In a question about best friends, I asked what quality made them **Best**. Here are some of the recurring attributes of a best friend:

- No secrets between us
- She is nonjudgmental
- She is a great listener

- She forgives my faults
- She is dependable
- We share common interests
- She is respectful
- We have chemistry
- Reliability—she is there for me
- We lift each other up
- I can confide in and vent to her
- She makes me laugh
- She finds the good in people
- She knows what I am thinking
- She has my back
- She doesn't fall for my crap
- She holds my feet to the fire
- She knows all of me
- Our conversation is effortless
- She won't share my secrets
- She makes me question myself, so I can grow
- She helps me feel comfortable in uncertainty
- She helps celebrate my wins
- She commiserates with me when I fail
- We don't give up on each other
- We share lots of history
- She is my cheerleader
- She is invested helping me level up
- She gives me space when I need to cry or just be silent
- She saved me when I was lost

- She is always there for me and drops everything to help me
- We laugh until we cry
- I can be completely myself with her
- We finish each other's thoughts
- She tells me what I don't want to hear when I need it
- She supports me even when she doesn't necessarily agree
- We have fun together
- She is like a family to me
- She checks on me
- She reminds me of my wisdom and power
- She makes an emotional investment in my life

Having a best friend is a blessing. Several of the respondents indicated that they have more than one best friend, and that is wonderful and something to strive for—a Tribe of BFFs. *BEST* isn't about exclusivity but rather years of stories, connection, and support granting the highest honor of friendship. Your Tribe is the best of the best. One person should not be responsible for getting all of your friendship needs met. A Tribe of best friends takes the pressure off.

When you have something going on and need support, no *one* person needs to feel completely responsible for being there. Somebody will be available and have your back. Each bestie adds her own background, skills, and personality. You get the best of all of their combined experience and exponential love. Some friends are good to go hiking with and others . . . shopping!

You can expect some great advice from different perspectives. Sometimes one can communicate something in just the right way, so you really hear it. One may hear your situation and share your frustration, validating your feelings. Another may suggest you look on the bright side and tell you everything coming your way is for your benefit, even if you don't see it now. Each of these viewpoints, although very different, IS helpful and comes from a place of love. More best friends just means more of everything—and I like MORE! More inside jokes, more adventures, more cheerleaders, more memories, and more to be grateful for.

Instant Friend Qualities

Respondents were asked: When meeting new people, what is it about someone that makes you want to be their friend immediately? Isn't this great insight for those of us looking to add to our Tribe? Here are some of the attributes that can speed up the friend courtship process.

- Open and approachable
- Authenticity
- Good sense of humor
- Their energy
- Common interests in music, art, or sports
- Their smile

- Charisma
- Intelligence
- A sense of grace
- How they treat others
- Gut feeling
- Nonjudgmental
- Warm personality
- Listening skills
- They enjoy life
- A kind heart
- Has life goals
- Active in the community, hobbies, or physically
- I feel their energy or vibe immediately—good or bad
- Easy to talk to, makes me feel comfortable
- Kindred spirit
- Asks interesting questions
- Looks me in the eyes when they talk
- They have a sparkle about them
- They are not fake
- Good conversationalist
- Not easily offended
- Similar values
- They share their story
- Not self-absorbed
- Positive outlook
- Thankful for blessings
- They break the ice and lead conversation
- Successful in some aspect of their life

- They like me for me
- Their demeanor
- Their confidence
- Being present in the moment

If you are in the market for new friends, the attributes listed above may be good to keep in mind. However, above all else be your authentic self. Don't try too hard to be congenial, appear intelligent, entertaining, or successful. The friendships you seek will like you and grow to love you for who you truly are.

The next couple questions of the survey dealt with friendship turnoffs. What situations are hard on a current friendship? What behaviors would repel someone from even getting to know somebody they have just met?

I have a hard time in friendship when . . .

There were a significant number of responses around the topic of reciprocity. Comments like "I am the one who always initiates—making time, calling, texting, inviting, or suggesting get-togethers." There are going to be points in our relationships when our efforts seem one-sided. Life *happens* to us all at different times, and on these occasions, friendships must push through continuing to reach out with support and connection. It's those relationships that seem always to be lopsided that are the problem.

Others commented: "They do all the talking; everything always has to relate to them, and the friendship is one way. It's all about them." I can understand completely why being on the receiving end of this behavior is difficult. Many of us have experienced being talked *at*. It is pretty amazing how someone can run on from one topic to the next almost without taking a breath and little opportunity for you to add an "ooh" or "ahh." Instead of the conversation being like a game of catch where the ball is passed back and forth, you are conversing with a ball hog who doesn't pass, shoots, and then rebounds the shot in an endless cycle.

I would like to believe most conversation hogs are the result of poor communication skills rather than just being completely self-absorbed. If you find yourself in this situation, you might try interjecting statements like, "I have something to add" or "Let's stop for a minute." Not all conversation hogs intend to dominate the conversation. They may be so passionate about the topic that they can hardly take a breath, let alone stop for input. These statements let them know that you have something to say and/or pauses them long enough to collect their thoughts, and they give you an opening to share your thoughts.

If you have a tendency to overshare and are often on the giving side of these downloads, be advised. We as humans like to be heard. There may be a relationship in your life where you don't feel heard, so you let it all out to anyone else who will listen. Be careful not to offer your download to the same person too often, or you may lose access to that friendship. They want to express themselves and be heard as well but may be too polite to interrupt. Instead, they will just stop taking your calls. This is one way that friendships grow apart, and you don't understand why.

Another respondent shared, "They aren't there for me as I am for them, and they take more than they give," which is another example of lack of reciprocity. Energy vampires, conversation hogs, and takers require direct feedback if the friendship is to survive. Your good manners and politeness can evolve into passive aggressive avoidance if this continues too long. If the friendship is important to you, let them know how you feel. A nonconfrontational way to initiate this conversation is to start with an "I feel . . ." statement. For example: "I feel unimportant when I hear all about the issue, and I don't have the opportunity to share my thoughts." It is hard for someone to argue with you about how you feel. The recipient will probably take a pause and consider the conversation. However, a statement like, "You talk all the time, and I can't get a word in edgewise!" will likely put the recipient in defense mode, and you may have an argument on your hands.

The road to friendship is a two-way street. Sometimes there may be periods when one has needs that require more attention and as tides turn, the other may need the same consideration. A friendship cannot thrive if it is one-sided or selfish in nature.

Lack of honesty was a deal breaker for many surveyed. When you don't feel you can trust a friendship, or that they may not have your best interests at heart, it's hard to maintain—let alone grow—the relationship. Gossip, betrayal, disloyal behavior, feeling judged, and political differences were all mentioned several times as friendship destroyers.

I have NO interest in developing a friendship when . . .

- Their talk and their walk don't match up—lack authenticity
- I feel negative energy
- They share personal info about someone else
- They talk in a hateful way
- They use racial slurs
- They dominate the conversation
- They create and attract drama
- They are rude to be funny
- They are selfish
- They are not open-minded
- They are critical, complain, or gossip about others
- They are dishonest
- They are late
- They are high maintenance
- They are disrespectful
- They are too superficial with social media
- They are overbearing or pushy
- They smoke
- They are a bully

It's sad to think that someone could strike out with only one encounter, but the poor etiquette described above would certainly do the trick! Many of these friend-repellent behaviors—such as elevating yourself by putting others down, being in the middle of drama to seem important, and sharing personal info or gossip to declare that you are in-the-know—are the result of one's insecurities. Sometimes our insecurities may make us behave out of character. As I said before, it is important to be yourself when meeting new people. Authenticity is the path to friendship.

The last question I would like to share from the Find Your Tribe survey is about strengthening our friendship branches. In our tree of life, our relationships are the trunk and branches that support our growth and help us flourish. Our branches can be strengthened with time and attention. I asked the respondents, "What are some of your favorite things your Tribe does for each other, or things you do together to strengthen your friendship?" Here are some of the highlights:

"We celebrate birthdays by planning an interesting outing that we think the birthday girl would love but wouldn't plan on her own (and her spouse probably wouldn't either). Sometimes we consult them; sometimes it's a surprise. We've gone to many unique places and had memorable experiences like: dinner theaters, hikes/picnics in the mountains, high teas at the Brown Palace and the Boulder Dushanbe Tea House. We've taken trips to the Botanic Gardens, the Denver Zoo, IMAX Theater, the Molly Brown House, the Colorado Natural History Museum, the Denver Art Museum, etc."

"We call ourselves the Gorgeous Gigglers. We realized that even though we have the connection of being healers at heart (which is how we met—in a healing circle), what keeps us strong is our ability to see each other's beauty through any of the ugliness we're trying to heal. We can always laugh together to get through adversity and really celebrate occasions."

"Picking up little things to make each other smile. Praying for each other and our kiddos. Just being there without words. We send flowers or schedule a last-minute Zoom call, socially distanced outdoor time, or brunch when someone needs it. Usually, everyone actually needs it. We walk and talk. We share when things aren't going well. We share with each other BEFORE posting on social media!"

"We know each other well enough to know when to check in and see if there's anything we can do to help. It might be a conversation, help with some kind of chore, or even financial help in hard times. We enjoy snail mail notes/cards, sharing big and small things that are happening, and walking life's journeys with one another that can only be done over time."

"We have brunch together and all contribute to the meal. We play games, drink, and enjoy each other's company. This is our time. If we have had a bad week, we can let it all out and commiserate together. If we need help with something, we have an open audience. We take some time together to get that reset done."

"When we have a girl's trip, even just a quick little night or two away, we all bring little gifts to share with each other. It's never a planned thing, but when we get to our destination, everyone has presents! Usually, the gifts are anywhere between $15 and $30. It's not that much, but it's such a sweet gesture and may have something to do with the trip we are on! I love that it's not planned and it naturally happens."

"We get together for a book club regularly. Instead of focusing on the book we have read, we end up spending the time catching up on our lives. One of my favorite times was when a bunch of us gathered at a local archery club to try our skills with bows and arrows! I also liked what Mrs. Wyoming did. She dressed up like a T-Rex and met her friends at the airport (they had flown in for a fun girl's weekend where they got all dressed up and went downtown)."

"We diet together, feast together, exercise together, lament together, and dissect why we can't diet and exercise together. It's all about the journey."

"We randomly send hello messages. That's it—'yo,' 'hey you,' 'dork,' or 'really?' Maybe the other responds, maybe not. Just random messages that say, 'I am thinking of you, want you to know, no pressure to act, and yeah . . . I still get you.' Birthdays are a big deal for us. We always make a point to celebrate with each other. We also just really work hard to get together whether it's for drinks, dinner, or just hanging out at someone's house.

Other activities shared include: going to the movies together, spending time away from kids, sending funny messages or sharing a social media post, game nights, escape rooms, axe throwing, and other new and different things.

One respondent only shared, "Not enough . . . . . I need to do more." That is okay. Acknowledging where you are right now is the first step! Deciding to do more is the next. You are already well on your way! I am so grateful to all of the people who took the time to share their friendship stats and stories on the Find Your Tribe Friendship Questionnaire. Although not scientific, the data revealed interesting trends. The stories were heartwarming and offered ideas we can all benefit from to enhance our own Tribe!

ACKNOWLEDGMENTS

I MUST START BY THANKING my amazing husband, Parker. He encourages me to go for it—whatever my heart desires—and he is always there to clear the way, so I can focus. I feel like he thinks I can do anything, and sometimes he convinces me that I can as well. I love you, Parker.

Ron and Norma (dad and mom), thank you for all of your hard work, dedication, and commitment to family, setting the stage for our charmed life. You are great role models for me, Bobbi, Brian, and your nine grandkids. I love you.

Thank you, mom, for stepping out of your comfort zone and agreeing to be the first to review my manuscript. You provided valuable feedback using your proofreading skills and even corrected me on some of my facts. Your encouragement helped me believe I was on the right track with this message.

Roseanne, you were so gracious to lend me your writing expertise in reviewing *Lady and the Tribe*. You offered some valuable insights and suggestions. You are very special to me.

I have the BEST mother-in-law in the world. I love you and thank you!

Parker Jr. and Gillian, thank you for being superstars in the things that you are passionate about. You inspire me to keep dreaming and "go after it." I love you, and I am so proud of you.

To my Tribe, Soul Sisters, and Kindred Clan, I love you. I don't think we knew what we were starting when we created space to be together, lean on, and be truly known by each other. We now know that girl time is not just about a fun night out. You complete me. Thank you!

Michelle, my Soul Seraph, thank you for writing such a lovely forward. I am honored by your blessing and introduction. Your kind heart and old soul are gifts to us all.

I am grateful to the Mrs. Colorado America organization for the opportunity to represent my community and become the best version of myself. The journey was incredible, and with the help of my coach, Alycia Darby, I found this book inside of me. The experience has been life changing. Thank you!

Thank you to my publishing team at My Word Publishing who eased my first time publishing overwhelm. Kiki Ringer—my concierge, counselor, and connector—orchestrated everything and pulled it all together. Laura Dent edited with a fine tooth comb and delivered her critique with grace. Victoria Wolf created the beautiful book cover that I am crazy about. Lauri Kane swept in like a super hero for a last minute proof. You are all amazing. Thank you.

Finally, I must thank my communities for their support and encouragement. My extended family, local networks, and social connections near and far: thank you for your likes, views, listens, and encouragement. It is scary putting yourself out there, and you all have been so supportive. I am grateful to have solid connections in each layer of my Friendship Target, complete but ever expanding.

Mandi,
Blessings to you and your Tribe!
♡ Brenda Ridgley

ABOUT THE AUTHOR

9/24/21

BRENDA RIDGLEY IS an author, speaker, and girlfriend guru who loves helping women connect, find success, and discover joy through friendship. Her mission is to start a movement: women coming together to build thousands of new Lady Tribes around the globe. Through her workshops, vlogs, blogs, and book clubs, Brenda helps women connect and communicate with respect, love, and trust. She holds an MA in human resources and has spent decades cultivating her own Tribe. A Colorado girl at heart, Brenda lives in the Carbon Valley area with her husband, Parker, two kids, Parker Jr. and Gillian, and pooch, Perry. She enjoys hiking and has conquered Longs Peak and several other 14'ers. To connect with Brenda, visit her website at www.BrendaRidgley.com.

Invite Brenda to speak at your next event:
Brenda@BrendaRidgley.com.

SUBSCRIBE:

 @BrendaRidgley

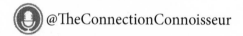 @TheConnectionConnoisseur

FOLLOW:

@BrendaRidgley

@BrendaRidgleyConnections

@BrendaRidgley

ENDNOTES

1   Monbiot, George, "The age of loneliness is killing us."
    The Guardian, (2014): https://www.theguardian.com/
    commentisfree/2014/oct/14/age-of-loneliness-killing-us

2   Tate, Nick, "Loneliness Rivals Obesity, Smoking as Health Risk."
    WebMD (2018): https://www.webmd.com/balance/news/20180504/
    loneliness-rivals-obesity-smoking-as-health-risk

3   Cigna, "Signs and Symptoms of Chronic Loneliness." Accessed
    August 31, 2021: https://www.cigna.com/individuals-families/
    health-wellness/chronic-loneliness

4   Hernandez, Dominic, "Your Social Life, Or Lack Thereof, Can
    Affect Your Health.", Texas A&M Today, (2018): https://today.tamu.
    edu/2018/06/26/your-social-life-or-lack-thereof-can-affect-your-
    health/

5   Tate, Nick, "Loneliness Rivals Obesity, Smoking as Health Risk."
    WebMD (2018): https://www.webmd.com/balance/news/20180504/
    loneliness-rivals-obesity-smoking-as-health-risk

6   Hernandez, Dominic, "Your Social Life, Or Lack Thereof, Can
    Affect Your Health.", Texas A&M Today, (2018): https://today.tamu.

edu/2018/06/26/your-social-life-or-lack-thereof-can-affect-your-health//

7   Hernandez, Dominic, "Your Social Life, Or Lack Thereof, Can Affect Your Health.", Texas A&M Today, (2018): https://today.tamu. edu/2018/06/26/your-social-life-or-lack-thereof-can-affect-your-health/

8   Campaign to End Loneliness, "The Facts on Loneliness," Accessed July 24, 2021: https://www.campaigntoendloneliness.org/the-facts-on-loneliness/

9   Cigna, "Signs and Symptoms of Chronic Loneliness." (2019): https://www.cigna.com/individuals-families/health-wellness/chronic-loneliness

10 PubMed.gov, "Biobehavioral responses to stress in females: tend-and-befriend, not fight-or-flight." Accessed July 24, 2021: https://pubmed.ncbi.nlm.nih.gov/10941275/

11 Pattee, Emma, "How to Have Closer Friendships (and Why You Need Them)", The New York Times, (2019): https://www.nytimes. com/2019/11/20/smarter-living/how-to-have-closer-friendships. html

12 Pattee, Emma, "How to Have Closer Friendships (and Why You Need Them)", The New York Times, (2019): https://www.nytimes. com/2019/11/20/smarter-living/how-to-have-closer-friendships. html

13 Dauven, Leiza, "When was the highest divorce rate?" AskingLot, (2020): https://askinglot.com/when-was-the-highest-divorce-rate

14 Lexico, Oxford English and Spanish Dictionary, "Definition of Friend", Accessed July 24, 2021: https://www.lexico.com/definition/friend

15 Wikipedia, "Definition of Frenemy" Accessed August 31, 2021: https://en.wikipedia.org/wiki/Frenemy

16 Urban Dictionary, s.v. "Definition of Frenemy," by Pipelayer35, Accessed July 24, 2021: https://www.urbandictionary.com/define. php?term=Frenemy

17 Oxford Learner's Dictionaries, "Definition of Friendship", Accessed July 24, 2021: https://www.oxfordlearnersdictionaries.com/ definition/english/friendship

18 TED: The Economics Daily, "Time spent in leisure activities in 2014, by gender, age, and educational attainment", U.S. Bureau of Labor Statistics, June 2015, Accessed July 24, 2021: https://www. bls.gov/opub/ted/2015/time-spent-in-leisure-activities-in-2014-by-gender-age-and-educational-attainment.htm

19 Beck, Julie, "How Friendships Change in Adulthood." The Atlantic, 2015, Accessed July 24, 2021: https://www.theatlantic.com/ health/archive/2015/10/how-friendships-change-over-time-in-adulthood/411466/

20 Beck, Julie, "How Friendships Change in Adulthood." The Atlantic, 2015, Accessed July 24, 2021: https://www.theatlantic.com/ health/archive/2015/10/how-friendships-change-over-time-in-adulthood/411466/

21 Shumway, Kyler, *The Friendship Formula*, Coppell, Kyler Shumway 2018

22 Encyclopedia.com, "Tribe." Accessed August 31, 2021: https://www. encyclopedia.com/social-sciences-and-law/anthropology-and-archaeology/anthropology-terms-and-concepts/tribe

23 Fuel, Amanda. Interview by Brenda Ridgley. In person Interview. Loveland, CO, July 23, 2021

24 McGinnis, Alan Loy, *The Friendship Factor*, Minneapolis, Augsburg Books, 1979

25 McDonald, Dick and Paula, *Loving Free*, New York City, Ballantine Books, 1974

26 Fox, Kate, "Girl Talk – The new rules of female friendship and communication." SIRC, Accessed July 24, 2021: http://www.sirc.org/publik/girl_talk.shtml

27 Cirino, Erica, "What are the Benefits of Hugging?" Healthline, (2018): https://www.healthline.com/health/hugging-benefits

28 Williamson, Marianne, *A Return to Love*, HarperOne, 1996

29 Griffin, Trudi, How to Know Who You Are." WikiHow, (2021): https://www.wikihow.com/Know-Who-You-Are

30 Law of attraction.com, "What Is The Law Of Attraction? Open Your Eyes To A World Of Endless Possibilities." Accessed August 31, 2021: https://www.thelawofattraction.com/what-is-the-law-of-attraction/

31 Leaver, Kate, "How many friends do we need to be happy?" ABC Everyday, (2020): https://www.abc.net.au/everyday/how-many-friends-do-we-need-to-be-happy/12589694

32 Leaver, Kate, "How many friends do we need to be happy?" ABC Everyday, (2020): https://www.abc.net.au/everyday/how-many-friends-do-we-need-to-be-happy/12589694

33 Degges-White, Suzanne, "How Many Friends Do You Really Need in Adulthood?" Psychology Today, (2019): https://www.psychologytoday.com/us/blog/lifetime-connections/201908/how-many-friends-do-you-really-need-in-adulthood

34 Weaver, Katie, "Iconic quotes from 'Sex and the City' to remind us of what's important."KRNL, (2020): https://www.krnlmagazine.com/post/iconic-quotes-from-sex-and-the-city-to-remind-us-of-what-s-important

35 Nelson, Shasta, *Frientimacy*, Berkeley, Seal Press, 2016

36 Hicks, Lyn. Interview by Brenda Ridgley. In person Interview. Longmont, CO, April 23, 2021

37 Wikipedia, "Numerology." Accessed on July 25, 2021: https://en.wikipedia.org/wiki/Numerology

38 Stubbings, Fiona, "How to build your tribe – the 6 friends every woman needs." Thrive Global, (2019): https://thriveglobal.com/stories/how-to-build-your-tribe-the-6-friends-every-woman-needs/

39 Stubbings, Fiona, "How to build your tribe – the 6 friends every woman needs." Thrive Global, (2019): https://thriveglobal.com/stories/how-to-build-your-tribe-the-6-friends-every-woman-needs/

40 Britannica, "Perfect number." Accessed on July 26, 2021: https://www.britannica.com/science/perfect-number

41 Dudley, Underwood, *Numerology: Or What Pythagoras Wrought*, Mathematical Association of America, 1997

42 The Free Dictionary by Farlex, "nowadays." Accessed July 25, 2021: https://www.thefreedictionary.com/nowadays

43 America's best pics & videos, Accessed July 25, 2021: https://americasbestpics.com/picture/never-blame-someone-else-for-the-road-you-re-on-QUKLZh5G8

44 Priority Matrix, "The Eisenhower Method: What is it?" Accessed July 25, 2021: https://appfluence.com/productivity/what-is-the-eisenhower-method/

45 Priority Matrix, "The Eisenhower Method: What is it?" Accessed July 25, 2021: https://appfluence.com/productivity/what-is-the-eisenhower-method/

46 Priority Matrix, "The Eisenhower Method: What is it?" accessed July 25, 2021, https://appfluence.com/productivity/what-is-the-eisenhower-method/

47 Hellman, Rick, "How to make friends? Study reveals time it takes" The University of Kansas, (2018): https://news.ku.edu/2018/03/06/study-reveals-number-hours-it-takes-make-friend

48   Patacchini, Eleonora, "How does geographical distance affect social interactions?" World Economic Forum, (2015) https://www.weforum.org/agenda/2015/07/how-does-geographical-distance-affect-social-interactions/

49   Cirino, Erica, "What are the Benefits of Hugging?" Healthline, (2018): https://www.healthline.com/health/hugging-benefits

50   Cirino, Erica, "What are the Benefits of Hugging?" Healthline, (2018): https://www.healthline.com/health/hugging-benefits

51   Lamberg, Erica, "What are the Benefits of Hugging, Backed by Science." The Healthy (2020): Health Benefits of Hugging, Backed By Science | The Healthy

52   James, Alfred, "15 Ways to Stop Energy Vampires Draining Your Life Source." Pocket Mindfulness, Accessed on July 25, 2021: https://www.pocketmindfulness.com/energy-vampires/

53   Lexico Oxford English and Spanish Dictionary, "Vulnerability", Accessed August 31, 2021: https://www.lexico.com/en/definition/vulnerability

54   Brown, Brene, *Daring Greatly: How the Courage to Be Vulnerable Transforms the Way We Live, Love, Parent, and Lead*, New York City, Avery Publishing, 2015

55   Gaspard, Terry, "5 Reasons Vulnerability Leads to a Long-Lasting Relationship & 4 Ways to Turn it into True Intimacy." Your Tango, (2020): https://www.yourtango.com/experts/terry-gaspard/5-top-reasons-why-being-vulnerable-leads-intimacy

56   Fuel, Amanda. Interview by Brenda Ridgley. In person Interview. Loveland, CO, July 23, 2021

57   Nelson, Shasta, *Frientimacy*, Berkeley, Seal Press, 2016

58   Hendricks, Drew, "Complete History of Social Media: Then And Now." Small Business Trends (2021): https://smallbiztrends.com/2013/05/the-complete-history-of-social-media-infographic.html

59 Hall, Mark, "Facebook." Britannica, 2021, Accessed on July 25, 2021: https://www.britannica.com/topic/Facebook

60 Wolpert, Stuart, "In our digital world, are young people losing the ability to read emotions?" UCLA Newsroom, (2014): https://newsroom.ucla.edu/releases/in-our-digital-world-are-young-people-losing-the-ability-to-read-emotions

61 Michigan News, "Empathy: College students don't have as much as they used to." Accessed July 25, 2021: https://news.umich.edu/empathy-college-students-don-t-have-as-much-as-they-used-to/

62 Siegler, MG, "Eric Schmid: Every 2 Days We Create As Much Information As We Did Up To 2003." Tech Crunch, (2010): https://techcrunch.com/2010/08/04/schmidt-data/

63 SlickText, "44 Smartphone Addiction Statistics for 2021." (2021): https://www.slicktext.com/blog/2019/10/smartphone-addiction-statistics/

64 Turkle, Sherry, "Alone but Connected." TED, (2012): https://www.ted.com/talks/sherry_turkle_connected_but_alone/up-next?language=en

65 Stopbullying.gov, "Facts About Bullying." Accessed July 27, 2021: https://www.stopbullying.gov/resources/facts

66 Maclin, Amy and Simms Molly, "How to Be a Better Friend in the Digital Age." Oprah Daily, (2019): https://www.oprahdaily.com/life/a28568922/how-to-be-a-better-friend-in-the-digital-age/

67 Seasons of Friendship, Accessed July 27, 2021: https://www.danceadts.com/newarticles/seasonsoffriendship.pdf and A Reason, A Season, A Lifetime, Accessed July 30, 2021: http://www.goldenproverbs.com/poems_reasonseason.html

68 Scripture taken from the New King James Version®. Copyright © 1982 by Thomas Nelson. Used by permission. All rights reserved.

69 wikiHow, "How to Keep a Secret." Accessed August 31, 2021: https://www.wikihow.com/Keep-a-Secret

70 Sasson, Remez, "The Journey of a Thousand Miles Begins with One Step." Success Consciousness, Accessed July 26, 2021: https://www.successconsciousness.com/blog-goalsetting/journey-begins-with-one-step/

71 Definitions, "Decision", Accessed August 31, 2021: https://www.definitions.net/definition/decision

72 Bond, Marybeth, "Women Travel Statistics from Women Travel Expert." Gutsy Traveler (2019): https://gutsytraveler.com/women-travel-statistics-women-travel-expert